Gary Fradin

Grandpa, What Did You Do During the Trump Years

Gary Fradin

Gary Fradin

All materials in this book are copyrighted © by Gary Fradin, 2021.
All rights reserved.
No part of this text may be reproduced
without the express written consent of Gary Fradin

The views expressed here are only those of the author.

To Ben and Isaac
who will live in the America we leave them

The world will not be destroyed by those who do evil
but by those who watch them without doing anything.
Albert Einstein

The pen is mightier than the sword.
Edward Bulwer-Lytton

Never argue with stupid people. They will drag you down to
their level then beat you with experience.
Mark Twain

Table of Contents

Preface and Introduction .... page 11

2018

Will Mental Health Background Checks Make Us Safer?... page 15

Thoughts and Prayers Are Not Enough............................. page 19

Canada's Outrageous Milk Subsidies (Not)....................... page 23

Foreign Policy Delusions.. page 25

Why I Worry About Tax Cuts.. page 27

Understanding Republican Economics.............................. page 29

'I' vs. 'We'.. page 33

America's Terrible Healthcare Non-System...................... page 37

Brigadoon Massachusetts, January 2072......................... page 39

Why I'll Vote 'No' On Question 1...................................... page 41

Who Believes Trump... page 43

The Harvard and Yale Impact... page 45

2019

Predications... page 47

Rex Tillerson Was Right... page 51

What I Learned About the US Senate in Alaska............... page 53

Chain Migration and Public Education Financing............ page 55

On Student Debt.. page 57

Economic Consequences.. page 59

Why Inequality Should Matter to You.............................. page 61

Cruelty as Public Policy... page 63

Thoughts on July 4... page 65
A Future of Hope or Fear... page 69
How to Save $27 Million in Local Taxes........................... page 71
Why Medicare for All Must Pass...................................... page 73
The Real Cost of Reducing Environmental Protections.... page 77
The Hypocrisy of Power.. page 79
Thoughts on a Long Walk Through Easton...................... page 81
Socialist Threats to America... page 83

2020

What the Democrats Get Wrong About Impeachment..... page 87
Political Definitions Today.. page 89
Compare, Contrast and Give Excuses................................ page 93
Beating Covid.. page 97
Saying Stop... page 101
Predicting the Presidential Election October Surprise...... page 105
I'm a Conservative... page 109
Why Black Lives Matter to Everyone................................ page 113
With All Due Respect.. page 115
Stealing Signs.. page 117
What Would Mussolini Say?... page 119
Protecting Pre-Existing Conditions?................................ page 123
Do Democrats Eat Their Old?... page 127
Has Our National Experiment Run It's Course?.............. page 129
Can Our House Divided Continue to Stand?................... page 133

The 'Republican Leaders' Oxymoron................................. page 137

2021

How NFL Coaches Might Explain Our Politics................... page 141

Epilogue, January 17, 2021

Can We Return 2021 Within 30 Days for a Refund?.......... page 143

Gary Fradin

Preface and Introduction

I felt physically ill when Donald Trump won the 2016 Presidential election. The values I held dear and world I had assumed suddenly shattered. Evil, I feared, had won the election.

I remember saying to my wife that night 'this will end badly' though exactly how and how badly was yet to unfold.

Unable to sleep and exhausted, the next morning I attended a professional business meeting. I remember feeling comforted by seeing the familiar faces of my colleagues, even those I disliked. It provided a semblance of normality.

As the Trump administration began, I attended marches, one after the next, for women, equality, justice and more. At each, impassioned speakers exhorted us to do something patriotic for America, to help the forces of good and decency overcome those of racism, hatred and tyranny.

What could I do? I was a small businessman, not wealthy, not politically skilled or connected and not terribly social. I disliked meetings and didn't want to 'organize', whatever that meant.

One day, my friend Craig Barger suggested writing Op Eds for our local town newspaper, the Easton Journal and introduced me to Donna Whitehead, the editor. 'Sure', she invited, 'submit some writing samples'.

I labored for hours over those test submissions. Op Ed writing is more difficult than it appears.

Apparently satisfied, the Journal published my pieces from 2018 – 2021. I became the Journal's unofficial liberal voice; they already had a conservative one.

My writing voice, style and focus evolved over time. Several 2018 pieces weren't too good; some in 2020 weren't too bad.

I don't know if my Op Eds changed any minds, promoted more thoughtful political discussions, helped defeat Trump in the 2020 election or ultimately had any impact on anyone. I hope so but suspect this exercise was ultimately more for me than for readers.

*****

Re my writing style. The Easton Journal is a local newspaper, more focused on town matters and high school sports than national issues. I decided that short summary pieces would fit their format and appeal to their readers more than long, detailed, footnoted ones.

Each article took me hours to write, reminding me of that famous author's lament 'I would have written less but I didn't have time'. Writing these renewed my admiration for playwrights, screen writers, journalists and other verbal efficiency professionals.

*****

Re quotes and data claims. As an overeducated pseudo-intellectual, I have footnotes for everything referenced here, all buried somewhere in my research notes.

*****

Re article order. These are grouped by year but not month since they often ran on a space available basis. The specific article order within each year here is entirely random.

*****

Re ending in January 2021. My purpose in writing these pieces – to promote sanity during the Trump administration's obnoxiousness – had disappeared with Joe Biden's election. I drafted the epilogue 'Can We Return 2021 Within 30 Days?' just before Biden' inauguration.

I don't know if I'll continue to write. The future is never foreseeable.

*****

Re: this book's title. Commentators often ask about their political opponents 'how will they explain that to their grandchildren?'.

This book is how I would answer if I had grandchildren.

2018

Gary Fradin

Will Mental Background Health Checks Make Us Safer?

Our current in-vogue gun control proposals focus on background checks aimed at depriving sick or bad people of the ability to buy guns.

They won't work for 2 main reasons.

First, social and psychological science is terribly weak at predicting the future actions of any specific individual; we simply don't know who to deprive of gun buying privileges.

Second, there are so many guns currently available on the secondary market that bad guys can get whatever they want, legally or otherwise, pretty much whenever they want it.

The net result of background checks: chest beating by some and perhaps a *slight* decrease in our national carnage rate but no great shakes.

Here's why:

Our current psychological and psychiatric science is pretty poor at predicting who will act out *before the event* even if it's pretty good at explaining why someone acted out *after the event*. We don't know in advance who – which individual - will become a murderer, let alone a mass murderer.

One study, for example, found a positive but very weak association between schizophrenia and violence: 35,000 patients with schizophrenia judged to be at high risk of violence would need to be detained in order to prevent 1 stranger homicide.

One in 35,000 is a pretty weak predictor.

Another study concluded that eliminating the risk of violence perpetrated by those with mental illness would still leave intact 96% of the violence that currently occurs in the general population.

96% is a pretty high remainder.

The best – although still poor - predictor of future violence among those diagnosed with mental illness is a constellation of risk factors including past violent behavior, juvenile detention, physical abuse, parental arrest record, substance abuse, age, sex, unemployment and a sense of victimization.

Correctly identifying any specific individual fitting that constellation who will become a murderer is like looking for the proverbial needle in a haystack: you get it wrong way more than you get it right, get harmed by mistakes pretty often and maybe never actually find the damn needle.

President Trump's idea of prohibiting gun purchases by the mentally ill thus begs the question of *which* mentally ill folks. All? That would likely stigmatize those in treatment and inhibit others from seeking it without actually accomplishing any gun carnage reduction - remember that 96% violence remainder estimate.

But this is all theoretical. What's the evidence on background checks and gun violence?

Massachusetts with a strong background check program, reported 242 firearm deaths in 2016, the most recent year available from the CDC.

Massachusetts has about 2% of the US population, meaning a national embrace of these background checks, at the Massachusetts firearm death rate, would still condemn over 10,000 Americans to firearm deaths annually.

I'd call that a programmatic failure.

But all of this misses the even bigger picture. There are already 300 million guns in the US including millions of semi-automatic assault rifles; 1 million AR-15s hit the streets in 2012 alone. The acquisition process on the secondary market is, according to the Sacramento Bee's investigation of it, 'relatively easy'.

So Devin Kelly – remember him from the Texas church massacre of 26 people in November, 2017? – Adam Lanza (Newtown shooter), Sayd Farook (San Bernadino) and James Eagan Holmes (Aurora,

Colorado) all could have acquired weapons or components pretty much whenever they wanted without much heavy lifting.

Mental health background checks serve more as political theater than substantive public policy.

Political theater consists of talk, posturing and fund raising.

Policy substance leads to fewer gun murders.

Mental health background checks won't ultimately save many lives.

If any at all.

Gary Fradin

Thoughts and Prayers are Not Enough

Our too-frequent school mass shootings – 228 since 2009 - all generate the same, almost scripted responses: stomach churning images on TV followed by thoughts and prayer statements about the victims in a Kabuki like performance.

Thoughts and prayer statements absent legislative solutions are political theater, not leadership.

Instead of vacuous words, here's the type of statement I'd like to see from our political leaders: 'America's school children are so important that I support legislation to ban assault weapons.'

Consider these two responses to the recent Parkland and Santa Fe school murders.

Representatives David Cicillini (D-R.I.) and Ted Deutch (D-Fla.) introduced legislation making it unlawful to 'import, sell, manufacture, transfer, or possess' an automatic or semiautomatic weapon. That's pretty clear, strong, unambiguous and appropriate.

On the other hand, President Trump stated that his administration will do 'everything in our power to protect our students' without actually saying what 'everything' means.

It clearly doesn't mean banning or restricting assault weapons. Trump made clear at the 2018 NRA convention that he opposes any dilution of Second Amendment rights.

'Everything' instead seems to mean blaming gun deaths on someone or something besides guns, like 'pure evil', whatever that is, the phrase Trump used after the Las Vegas concert massacre of 50 people.

He's is not alone in this. The Republican school safety program, vague though it is, apparently consists of arming school guards and limiting the number of school entrances as Texas Lieutenant Governor Dan Patrick proposed after the Santa Fe shooting: 'There are too many entrances and too many exits' at public schools, he said. 'There aren't enough people to put a guard at every entry.'

Aside from the tragedy of turning public schools into armed camps, this would do nothing to protect non-school victims like the 14 dead San Bernardino public health workers in 2015, the 49 Orlando nightclubers in 2016 or the 58 Las Vegas concert goers in 2017.

Nor the hundreds of wounded at these and other shootings.

Does 'everything in his power' include national background checks prior to gun purchase? No, but they wouldn't work anyway. Mental health status is a notoriously poor predictor of gun violence and Dimitrios Pagourtzis, the Santa Fe shooter, would have passed.

And, since we already have millions of assault weapons available on the secondary market, anyone who wants one can get one regardless of mental health or other status.

Background checks will do to mass shootings about what marijuana laws did to pot access over the past 40 years - pretty much nothing.

No, rather than protect school kids, concert goers and all the others, Trump and his Republican allies shirk responsibility by hiding behind the Constitutional guarantees from the same Constitution that aims to ensure domestic tranquility and promote the general welfare. Widespread access to assault weapons supports neither of those goals.

I'd be wary of relying on strict Constitutional arguments because the Constitution writers goofed a few times, like when they determined that African Americans were 3/5 of a person. We evolved from that huge mistake. Why not from the out-of-date Second Amendment?

The right to keep and bear arms probably made sense in the agrarian society of 1787 that felt threatened by the outside force of Great Britain – correctly so, as the War of 1812 demonstrated.

But we're no longer an agrarian, frontier economy and we aren't facing a potential invasion. We're a knowledge based country with a strong and sophisticated military. The musket ownership justification of 1787 simply doesn't fit the assault weapon reality of 2018.

I'd like to see the Second Amendment modernized if not eliminated. A 21st century approach would ban automatic and semiautomatic weapons and include a mandatory government buy-back, more or less eminent domain for weapons. Reimburse owners for their (previously legal) purchases, get assault weapons off the streets and make us safer.

That's what the Presidential oath of office - to 'preserve, protect and defend the Constitution' – requires. Focus on the reasons we have a Constitution, the domestic tranquility and general welfare bits.

Then reconsider the 228 school shootings in the past 9 years and ask yourself if hope and prayer without an assault weapons ban promotes the general welfare. I think not.

I hope Trump and the Republicans can honor all their Constitutional responsibilities, not to mention moral imperatives, and stop these regular shootings.

That would certainly help make American great again.

Gary Fradin

Canada's Outrageous Milk Subsidy (Not)

"Canada charges the US a 270% tariff on Dairy Products." shrieked President Trump's twitter last June 8. "Not fair to our farmers."

True.

And misleading.

Here's why.

US domestically produced milk is extremely low cost compared to the rest of the world. Compare a gallon of milk in June, 2018 as estimated by the Expatistan website:

- Boston $3.16
- London $4.93
- Paris $5.53
- Toronto $5.00

Prices reflect national political and economic priorities and answer questions like 'should we subsidize our domestic dairy industry?' or 'should we subsidize milk consumers?' or 'should we let the market determine prices?' Each country makes its own decision.

In the US, we choose to support dairy farmers in two main ways. First we subsidize corn production, corn being the primary food source for cows in industrialized farms, by about $5 billion per year.

That keeps our milk production costs below the world average and Canada's.

Second, we subsidize dairy delivery costs by taxing gasoline less than other countries, taxes being the largest component of gas prices and trucks being a key milk transportation mode. Consider Bloomberg's May 2018 estimates per gallon:

- US $2.99
- Canada $4.45

- Britain $6.59
- France $6.99

All this means US taxpayers keep domestic milk prices artificially low.

Canadians look at this and say 'Good for you Americans.

But we choose not to subsidize corn and gas. Instead we'll let the market determine milk prices.

To offset your subsidies that keep milk prices artificially low, we need to tax American milk imports so they cost the same as Canadian domestic products.

We don't want *your* farm subsidies to destroy *our* dairy industry.'

Unfair to American farmers?

The correct question, it seems to me, is 'unfair to American taxpayers?' I don't drink much milk but subsidize it through my taxes.

I, like millions of other Americans, subsidize American dairy farmers.

And that, in a nutshell, is why we'll apparently go to (trade) war with Canada.

Foreign Policy Delusions

Trade wars are good and easy to win according to Donald Trump.

His foreign policy ostensibly favors bilateral negotiations over multinational arrangements.

We've exited the Paris Climate Accords and Trans Pacific Partnership, threatened to leave NAFTA and verbally diminished the G7, all to be replaced, at least theoretically, with individual, post-trade-war-victory bilateral agreements that enhance America's interests.

Not so fast.

Trade wars are harder to win today than they may have appeared decades ago. Compare our relative economic power in 1960 and today.

In 1960 the US accounted for around 38% of the world's total economy. In other words, our Gross Domestic Product was about 38% of the Gross World Product.

Here were the biggest economies in 1960 when trade wars were presumably easy to win:

- US 38% of Gross World Product
- United Kingdom 5% of GWP
- France and China 4.5% of GWP each

Post 1960, other country's economies grew. They became markets for our goods, which in turn, stimulated our own growth.

At the same time, the world organized itself into international economic groupings like the European Union, which sometimes acts as an integrated economic entity.

Today we only account for 15% of Gross World Product according to CIA public data.

The Big Three today are:

- China 18% of Gross World Product
- US 15% of GWP
- European Union 15% of GWP

This strikes me as the wrong time to start a trade war and embrace Trump's 'we're America, bitch' foreign policy. (Yes, that's a direct quote from a Trump advisor reported in the Atlantic and New York Times.)

Trade wars may have looked smart in 1960 when we could pick on countries that were smaller and weaker than us.

But they look dumb today when we pick on entities our own size or bigger.

Teddy Roosevelt put the economic power idea succinctly: Speak softly and carry a big stick.

Donald Trump's version is more like: Shriek, and then if you don't get your way, shriek some more.

Starting a trade war today looks like unhinged megalomaniacal nostalgia which, I fear, bodes badly for us.

Why I Worry About Tax Cuts

Tax cuts, our Republican friends tell us, stimulate so much economic growth that the government takes in the same amount or even more money after the cuts, albeit at a lower marginal tax rate.

Ronald Reagan believed this as did both George Bushes and Donald Trump. All cut taxes during their administrations.

And all left us deeper in debt as a result, meaning our kids face increasingly huge debt repayment responsibilities as a result.

That's the problem with the theory. It never actually works out in real life.

Here's the gory history going back to 1980:

Ronald Reagan took office with a US national debt of $908 billion. Several tax cuts later, he left office with a $2,602 billion federal debt.

George H. W. Bush followed, promised no new taxes, pretty much delivered and drove the national debt to $4,065 billion.

Another way to look at the Reagan and H.W. Bush 12-year period: Our Federal debt grew from 32% of GDP to an astonishing 62%.

George W. Bush's tax cuts added more, pushed the debt up to 68% of GDP and left us owing a whopping $10,025 billion.

And a deep recession.

Obama dealt with that recession pretty well so eight years later Donald Trump took over a healthy economy with the stock market at record highs and unemployment near record lows.

Instead of repaying any of this huge debt, he lowered taxes.

2018 will end with a federal debt of around $21,478 billion or 107% of GDP.

Interest payments alone run north of $270 billion per year at our current historically low interest rates. I hate to think of what happens if interest rates double. (They were about 5x higher in 1980.)

All this raises a fundamental question: Do Republicans actually care about debts and the burden they place on our kids?

I suspect not.

In fact, I suspect Republican elected officials are so dependent on business lobbies for campaign contributions that they actually believe the 'tax cuts stimulate economic growth and therefore greater government income' theory despite the clear historical contradictory record.

I see this less as intentional deviousness and more as a modern incarnation of Sinclair Lewis's brilliant aphorism, slightly modified here to 'it's difficult to get a politician to understand something when his campaign contributions depend on his not understanding it.'

Republicans, it seems to me, believe that past tax cuts failed to generate the promised government tax benefits each for some idiosyncratic reason: unanticipated oil price increases, Icelandic bank failures, poor targeting and implementation or the like, but not because this is a fundamentally flawed approach.

This time, they always seem to believe, it's different.

But it never is. The net result is always the same: more debt burden for our kids and grandchildren and more fiscal risk to the US.

The next time Republicans call for tax cuts that pay for themselves, remember the history. Stop trying to achieve the historically unachievable.

The next time *won't* be different.

Have some pity on our kids who will have to pay for all these errors.

Understanding Republican Economics

I attended this year's Massachusetts Democratic State Convention and heard speaker after speaker assail our current terrible economy.

Terrible economy? We have 3 ½ percent unemployment, record corporate earnings and a strong stock market.

What's so terrible?

It turns out there are 2 different but equally important ways to view our economy: how well it produces goods and services, and how well it distributes them.

Republicans focus on how well we make stuff, sometimes called economic efficiency.

We're really good at this. Just look at the bounty available in our supermarkets and the technology in today's cars.

Then remember that food and car costs have gone *down* over time as a percentage of average family income.

Kudos to us.

Democrats, on the other hand, focus on distribution or how easily our citizens can access these wonderful goods and services. We pretty bad at this with millions of us seeking affordable housing, good public transportation and safe neighborhoods.

Consider these gory numbers:

Nationally half of American households (average size 2.5 people) earn less than $70,000, sometimes way less; the average Latino American household earns only $40,000.

Locally, 87% of Brockton public school students live below the Federal Poverty Level of $20,000 for a family of 3. That strikes me as outrageous.

Which is more important, production efficiency or distribution equity? We clearly need both, but when given a choice like at next

November's elections, I'll choose distributive equity for 3 main reasons:

First, that's the government's historical function. The private sector's is efficiency and our private sector's already plenty good at this.

Second, equitable distribution strengthens the demand side of our economy's 'supply and demand' function. If we, together, can get help Brockton kids become middle class, they'll buy more of the goods and services we produce in the future.

That's great for our long term economic growth.

Third, somewhat surprisingly, the greater our public investments and the less our economic inequality, the healthier we're each likely to be and the longer we're each likely to live. Extensive research over the past 30 years suggests that relative economic deprivation is a coronary disease risk factor and a life shortening one.

More inequality, in other words, leads to shorter lives.

And not just for the poor.

Rich Americans, according to research, live less long than similarly rich people in other countries due, at least in part, to our choice of efficiency-focused tax cuts over equity-oriented investments in public health programs, mass transit systems and the like.

Today we have more cars on the roads than ever – because we're so good at making them - leading to longer, more stressful commutes that take a longevity toll on even the wealthiest among us.

And our desire for never-ending tax cuts robs us of fast, efficient mass transit which, in turn, makes it more difficult for those low income Brocktonians to get jobs on 128 or in Boston and join the middle class.

Too many tax cuts and too much economic efficiency, in other words, is counterproductive.

That's the fundamental problem with Republican economics: we're so efficient that the system breaks down.

That harms each of us personally, our economy generally, our social fabric and our health.

Looks like bad policy to me.

Gary Fradin

'I' vs. 'We'

Republicans and Democrats frame public policy fundamentally differently. Republicans focus on 'I'; Democrats on 'we'.

Republicans, first, prize individual accomplishment, often summarized as 'I bought this house' or 'I built this business' (or in the future tense, 'I'm going to build my own business.'), thanks to hard work, sacrifice, determination and the like.

The paradigm Republican statement 'I worked 12 hours a day, six days a week for years to achieve all this' implies that anyone with similar character putting forth similar effort could have done the same.

This thinking leads to three political positions:

First, eliminating high taxes and excessive regulations, both barriers to success, helps others achieve similarly to yourself.

Second, people who don't succeed fail due to personal shortcomings: they're just not good, upstanding and hardworking enough. Specific examples of people who rose from underprivileged roots to business success reinforces this thinking.

Third, these two merge into 'I don't want to give away the fruits of my labors to undeserving people,' like welfare moms, poor English speaking immigrants and others of whose low character precludes them from investing the effort necessary to improve their economic condition.

No wonder Republicans oppose immigration. They see hordes of people coming to live off of them.

And no wonder Republicans support gun rights. They have to defend all that they've achieved from the underserving people trying to take it away. 'I may have to take things into my own hands' mirroring their idealized approach to success in the first place.

Democrats completely disagree and focus on 'we': 'If we, as a society, do well, then I'll do just fine.'

Democrats see personal success as a combination of background, resources, supports *and* personal effort. It takes a family, a school system, peer group and more – a village in short – to promote widespread individual successes.

In my own case, I grew up in a middle-class town not unlike Mansfield or Easton, attended excellent public schools, had an aspirational peer group, lots of role models, financial stability and engaged, motivated parents. From that basis and a couple graduate degrees, I did pretty well.

Of course I studied and worked hard – that goes without saying. But the surprise would have been <u>not</u> to have achieved.

Ditto for my kids and their cohort.

Contrast this with kids living in the Brocktons or Springfields of our state: poor quality schools, unsafe neighborhoods, few role models, little aspirational support, no financial stability and little help navigating our hugely complicated higher education and financial landscape.

Of course their average achievement lags.

Rather than seeing this growing underclass as victims of their own low character, Democrats see both a tragedy and opportunity.

The tragedy is for those who miss out in their own lives.

The opportunity is to improve our society overall. If Brockton produced as many doctors and engineers per capita as Easton, then all of us would benefit.

Democrats predicate on 'we': if we all do well, then I'll do just fine. They see the government as a force for good that improves public education, protects the environment, reduces inequality and provides the infrastructure that our entire society needs to grow and prosper.

Republicans predicate on 'I': if I do well, then anyone can and everyone of good character will. They see the government as an obstacle to individual success that takes their money, interferes with business growth and subsidizes the undeserving.

The I vs. We chasm looks unbreachable in the short term.

I hope it's not in the long term.

Gary Fradin

America's Terrible Healthcare Non-System

A healthcare system, at minimum, keeps people alive.

A good one keeps them alive longer.

A really good one keeps them alive longer at lower costs.

Ours is terrible. It keeps us alive shorter than other advanced countries and does so at the highest costs in the world.

Compare us to Spain, for example. We spend over $10,000 per capita on healthcare annually, they about $3300. Spaniards live 83.1 years on average and rising; we 78.6 and falling slightly.

Their 3 1/2 year longevity advantage is expected to grow to 6 years by 2040 even though we'll continue to outspend them by a ton.

Why?

The core, fundamental reason was articulated by Andrew Dreyfus, CEO of Blue Cross of Massachusetts in the Boston Globe last June: American healthcare is designed around the needs of institutions like hospitals, and health professionals like doctors and nurses, not around the needs of patients.

Patients get too much care that doesn't work and too little that does.

Consider beta blockers for example, blood pressure lowering drugs of which atenolol is most common. Atenolol registered 30 million prescriptions in 2016.

Extensive research shows that beta blockers make little to no difference in the number of heart attacks or deaths.

A blood pressure lowering drug that doesn't prevent heart attacks or death, prescribed 30 million times annually in the US? Yes, really. Happy to provide references.

Or knee surgery to treat osteoarthritis. We've known since the early 2000s that it's no more effective than a placebo procedure but Americans get thousands of these surgeries every year.

And so on. Estimates run to $800 billion or more annually of care that doesn't benefit patients.

We also get too little care that actually extends our lives. Consider the recent Journal of the American Medical Association study showing that a lack of regular exercise increases your mortality risk by about 390%, making it arguably worse than smoking.

Not particularly eye-opening: we've known this in broad outline for decades.

But do American patients routinely get exercise prescriptions, oversight and monitoring from doctors? No.

Does our healthcare system offer regular, ongoing, incentivized, long term exercise programs for all? No.

Instead when the lack of exercise shows up in patients 'numbers', they get atenolol prescriptions.

Who's to blame for all this? Everyone in my opinion, including **you**, the patients who take these ineffective drugs and agree to these ineffective treatments.

Until and unless patients – you - stop accepting ineffective care, we'll way overspend on medical care.

Until and unless patients – you again - demand a system that encourages exercise, we'll way underperform Spaniards, Canadians, Japanese, Danes and others on longevity measures.

So here's a 2-step process for improving healthcare:

- First, stop accepting non-beneficial treatments. Unfortunately, it's harder to do than you might think.
- Second, if you want to live a long time, go for a walk.

That, for better or worse, is the best any of us can do to cut healthcare spending and improve our life expectancies.

Somewhat surprisingly though, it's a lot!

Brigadoon, Massachusetts
January 1, 2072
From our correspondent Rip Van Fradin

I recently awoke from a 50-year slumber and find myself in the Republic of New England.

My neurologist says the slumber was a coping mechanism: the last thing I remember was calling the phone company for plan prices, asking if 15 minutes could save me 15% and then losing 15 pounds for $15 plus the cost of food.

The Republic of New England formed following the political and economic collapse of the United States in 2021. President Kamala Harris tried to reconstruct the old federal system but her predecessor Donald Trump had so weakened governmental institutions and public trust that Harris failed.

The Founding Mothers, led by Elizabeth Warren, Gina Raimondo, Jean Shaheen and Maura Healy, established the Republic of New England based on their shared vision of universal healthcare, free higher education, social equality and a pollution free environment.

New Englanders today enjoy the highest standards of living in North America with household incomes 50% higher than in the Fly Over Republic to the west.

Life expectancies similarly exceed Fly Over by 11 years. Most people attribute this to the high-quality healthcare system, enlightened social and environmental policies, fruit and vegetable subsidies and junk food sales taxes.

The obesity rate here, just 7% of the population, is a full 40% lower than in Fly Over.

New England offers free public higher education to all qualified residents. An astonishing 70% of 24-year olds hold bachelor's or other advanced degrees. None have any student debt.

This high quality, free education is funded largely by foreign students – 40% of the student body - paying full costs.

Indeed, many native New Englanders marry foreign students who choose to settle here. The liberal immigration policies bring a cultural vibrancy to the region in addition to strong connections in many foreign countries, a key component of solid economic growth for the past several decades.

This dynamic knowledge-based economy is fueled almost entirely by renewable energy from off-shore wind farms and Canadian hydropower. The cost/kilowatt hour here is about 1/3 that of the Shenandoah Valley where clean (dirty) coal remains the primary fuel source and upper respiratory disease medical costs equal public education spending.

New England's strong economy has attracted so-called 'undesirable' immigrants, primarily from the Shenandoah Republic states of Kentucky and West Virginia. A recent 'build a wall to keep them out' movement headed by David Dennison, hero of the Stormy Daniels nor'easter covfefe, made headlines.

Dennison doesn't want these poorly educated, lazy, unhealthy people living off hard working New Englanders but his movement has very few supporters.

New Englanders have enjoyed watching 95-year old Tom Brady lead the Patriots to 52 straight AFC championships. Tom recently signed a new 5-year contract that includes season ticket for his grandchildren.

I'm seriously considering another long nap.

*****

2021 explanations:

'David Dennison' was Trump's pseudonym in a non-disclosure agreement with Stormy Daniels to cover up an extra-marital affair.

'Covfefe' was Trump's apparent misspelling of 'coverage' ('press coverage') in a 2017 tweet. It became an internet meme.

Joe Biden, not Kamala Harris, won the 2020 Presidential election.

Why I'll Vote No on Question 1

I like nurses. They've treated me and my family extremely well when we've been hospitalized. They perform invaluable services and, in my experience, typically incredibly well.

But I dislike state healthcare staffing mandates. That's why I'll vote 'no' on Question 1.

Mandates reflect the political power of an interest group to get favorable treatment for its members.

In general, healthcare interest groups seek staffing mandates when they can't achieve their goals through private sector negotiations.

The nurse's union wants hospitals to hire more nurses and pay them more. That's why unions exist, to protect member interests. Hospitals balk, so the nurse's union tries to enlist public support by convincing voters that having more nurses, with the related higher medical spending, somehow serves the public interest.

But the nurse's union doesn't reflect the public interest any more than the X-ray technician union, physician union, hospital cleaner union, hospital food staff union or any other! They exist to benefit their own members.

Should we mandate minimum levels of these and thousands more staffing functions?

Consider history: the US had 7 state healthcare mandates in 1965 but over 1800 in 2016. During that time period, healthcare spending per capita rose from about $1700 to $10,000 in constant 2016 dollars.

The various mandate-supported groups did well.

But life expectancy – increasing it being the real goal of our healthcare system - only rose 9 years and most of that, according to Harvard professors Rashi Fein and Jules Richmond among others, was attributable to improved public health programs.

No research that I've read, and I study this stuff for a living, has pointed to mandated hospital staffing requirements as impacting life expectancy trends.

That's why I oppose staffing mandates in general.

I oppose this question for 2 specific reasons:

First, I have no idea how many patients each nurse should treat. And neither do other voters. We – voters - are the wrong group to decide.

Second, I have no idea how future medical technology improvements will affect the patient-to-nurse ratio. But codifying a specific ratio in law today may negate the benefits of such future technology improvements tomorrow.

There is a much better way to address hospital staffing questions: track patient outcomes from each hospital. Publish quarterly risk-adjusted patient mortality, infection, discharge and readmission rates by medical condition, by hospital.

That real time (or as real time as we can get in healthcare) information will tell hospitals how well they're actually doing, where they're outstanding and where they fall behind. It will give hospitals the information necessary to improve patient care.

And patients, now armed with care quality information, can choose the best hospital for their needs.

This kind of patient outcome data is sorely needed in our healthcare system. It is, in my opinion, the most critical missing component.

If you really want to improve healthcare, require hospitals to publish risk adjusted patient outcome data by medical condition.

Mandating that would be an excellent step and one I could get behind.

But not Question 1. It's just a financial and power grab by one specific union.

Who Believes Trump?

We know pretty well who believes President Trump's factually challenged assertions, statements like millions of Californians voted many times in the recent mid-term elections.

They're largely non-college educated, white, rural folks. That's pretty clear from voting maps.

The interesting question, though, is why this particular demographic group believes Trump's blatantly false assertions.

Erich Fromm, a psychoanalyst, suggests that psychological attachment theory offers some useful insights here.

People, according to Fromm, develop different kinds of attachments, or 'bonds', to each other. Primary bonds attach a child to a parent, the person who makes them feel safe in the world.

As people grow and develop, they separate from those primary bonds and develop new sources of emotional support with, say, a spouse, church or business, still to make themselves feel secure. That's normal, healthy human development.

But the outside world may interfere. The economy may preclude economic security. Evolving societal norms can feel threatening.

Consider conservative rural areas today. They've lost economic power to cities. Gay marriage and trans-sexual rights threaten traditional beliefs. Immigrants compete for jobs.

The world ain't what it used to be; it's less safe and secure.

Fromm suggests that this may entice people to develop unhealthy secondary bonds with an authority figure in an attempt to recreate the safety they once felt: "the frightened individual seeks for somebody or something to tie his self to...to feel security again".

Enter Donald Trump. He's an authority figure who can satisfy that emotional need. His factually challenged statements provide comfort and explain why evil liberals, Democrats, gays and immigrant-lovers win elections; they cheat.

The complete lack of evidence, rather than invalidating the statements, shows how well they cheated. Again, emotional satisfaction.

See Mueller's Russia probe in this light. It's far less a legal investigation than an emotional threat to Trump supporters.

In Fromm's terms, Mueller feels like the childhood acquaintance who says 'my dad makes more money than yours,' provides the evidence and leaves you feeling injured. Unacceptable to people who have attached themselves to Trump for emotional security reasons.

But Fromm didn't write about re-establishing unhealthy secondary bonds to describe Donald Trump.

Instead, he wrote Escape from Freedom in 1942 to explain Hitler's rise to power. How could an advanced, educated population, Fromm asked, discard civilized behavior and subjugate itself to a madman?

His answer: secondary bonds to a strong authority figure. Hitler offered emotional support to people who felt gipped by life.

These secondary bonds are so strong and unhealthy that

> When Fascism came into power, most people were unprepared… They were unable to believe that man could exhibit such propensities for evil, such lust for power, such disregard for the rights of the weak, or such yearning for submission.

Update to Trump's America. Truth isn't truth, says his lawyer. Alternative facts are facts, says his advisor. "I alone can fix it," says Trump himself.

His supporters cheer and feel safe once again.

That's the emotional power of authoritarian secondary bonds for the angst-filled among us.

I find Fromm's insights useful.

I wish I could say they are wrong.

The Harvard and Yale Impact

We're an egalitarian society in which any kid can, according to lore, grow up to become President of the United States.

But we're an elitist society when you look at who actually runs for President on both the Democratic and Republican tickets.

Consider the Presidential candidates over the past 30 years. Of the 8 elections since 1988, meaning 16 Presidential candidates from the two major parties, only 2 didn't attend Ivy League schools and only 3 didn't attend Harvard or Yale.

- 1988: George H.W. Bush (Yale) vs. Michael Dukakis (Harvard Law)
- 1992: Bill Clinton (Yale Law) vs. H.W. Bush
- 1996: Clinton vs. Bob Dole (Washburn University)
- 2000: George W. Bush (Yale and Harvard Business School) vs. Al Gore (Harvard)
- 2004: W. Bush vs. John Kerry (Yale)
- 2008: Barak Obama (Harvard Law) vs. John McCain (US Naval Academy)
- 2012: Obama vs. Mitt Romney (Harvard Law and Business Schools)
- 2016: Donald Trump (University of Pennsylvania Wharton Business School) vs. Hilary Clinton (Yale Law)

81% of our Presidential candidates since 1988 attended either Harvard or Yale.

Now consider some likely Democratic candidates in 2020. (I assume Donald Trump will run again on the Republican side.)

Of the 9 Democrats most likely to win the nomination as of November, 2018 according to Ladbrokes, the London bookie, 6 have Ivy League connections including 4 from Harvard or Yale. Here they are in descending odds order:

- Kamala Harris (Howard University)
- Beto O'Rourke (Columbia)
- Elizabeth Warren (Harvard Law professor)

- Joe Biden (University of Delaware)
- Bernie Sanders (University of Chicago)
- Amy Klobuchar (Yale)
- Cory Booker (Yale Law)
- Kristin Gillibrand (Dartmouth)
- Michael Bloomberg (Harvard Business School)

I certainly wouldn't place any bets here: neither Donald Trump nor Barak Obama would have headed their own party's favorites list 2 years before their elections.

But I can't figure out why Harvard and Yale continue to display such a disproportionate influence.

I doubt that their students are smarter than Stanford, Duke, MIT or Carnegie-Mellon folks or more driven than Georgetown, Michigan, Berkley or Rice graduates, to name just a few of many excellent American universities.

But I think it's odd. In an economy and country as diverse as ours, leaders should come, at least statistically, from lots of different backgrounds and universities.

Historically, you didn't have to attend Harvard or Yale to become President: Eisenhower, Johnson, Nixon, Carter and Reagan didn't.

But since 1988, almost all our Presidents and contenders have.

I guess today's message is that if you want to become President of the United States, you don't have to attend Harvard or Yale....

But it certainly seems to help.

2019

Predictions

Now that 2019 has actually started let's make some predictions.

The downside of writing these publicly, of course, is that my predictive abilities will be on view to all next December.

Join me and write down your own answers. Let's see who, if any of us, should consider fortune-telling as a next career.

Several of these questions have more than 1 right answer. You can find mine at the bottom.

1. How many electricity outages will Easton suffer in 2019?

    a. 1
    b. 5
    c. 10
    d. 20

2. How many snow days will the Easton schools have in the winter of 2019?

    a. 1
    b. 5
    c. 10
    d. 20

3. Which of the following Patriots will not return for the 2019-2020 season?

    a. Tom Brady
    b. Rob Gronkowski
    c. Bill Belichik
    d. Josh McDaniels

4. How far will the Red Sox go in 2019?

    a. Not make the playoffs
    b. Lose in the Division rounds
    c. Lose in the Conference round
    d. Lose the World Series

     e. Win the World Series
5. How far will the Celtics go in 2019?

    a. Not make the playoffs
    b. Lose in the first round of the playoffs
    c. Lose in the second round of the playoffs
    d. Lose in the Conference final
    e. Lose in the NBA final
    f. Win the NBA title

6. Which of the following people will get indicted in 2019?

    a. Donald Trump Jr.
    b. Jared Kushner
    c. Ivanka Trump
    d. Donald Trump
    e. All of the above

7. Who will be President of the United States on December 31, 2019?

    a. Donald Trump
    b. Mike Pence
    c. Chuck Grassley
    d. Hillary Clinton (sorry, typo)

8. Which of the following will not announce a Presidential run in 2019?

    a. Joe Biden
    b. Beto O'Rourke
    c. Cory Booker
    d. Jeff Flake
    e. None of the above; they'll all announce

9. What will the Dow Jones Industrial Average be on December 31, 2019?

    a. 3200
    b. 2800
    c. 2400

d. 2000

10. What will Robert Mueller's report say?

    a. The Trump campaign's relations with various Russian operatives had little to no impact on the 2016 election outcome
    b. The Trump organization was entirely financed by Stormy Daniels' tips
    c. The Trump organization laundered billions of dollars of Russian money
    d. The Trump organization and Trump campaign broke no US laws

11. What will Hillary Clinton do in 2019?

    a. Write another book that no one will read
    b. Learn to knit
    c. Attempt another Presidential campaign despite loud groans from the entire country
    d. Divorce Bill and marry the only fan she still has, Michael Moore

12. What will be the biggest story in Easton in 2019?

    a. The Lions Club will be named the Most Outstanding Lions Club in the World for the 2nd time since 2000
    b. The basketball, football, cross country and track teams will all win State titles
    c. Easton and Mansfield merge politically to gain power in the state senate and house
    d. Whatever happens in your own family is far more important than anything else

My answers: 1 (b), 2 (b), 3 (b), 4 (c), 5 (d), 6 (e), 7 (a), 8 (e), 9 (b), 10 (c), 11 (c), 12 (d)

Gary Fradin

Rex Tillerson Was Right

Rex Tillerson ran Exxon for 11 years then became US Secretary of State. He regularly met business and world leaders.

His assessment of Donald Trump?

Trump's a moron.

Let me count the ways.

First, Trump kept the US out of the Trans Pacific Partnership, an economic alliance of Pacific Rim countries. That raised prices of American products like beef, pork and wheat in Japan, Australia and others, directly harming those industries; American beef, for example, now pays a 38% tariff in Japan while Australian falls to 9%.

Simultaneously, Trump's decision ceded Rim economic and political leadership to China.

We lost money and power for no upside.

Moron!

Second, he moved the US embassy to Jerusalem, a long held Israeli dream, without getting anything in return. He could have demanded an end to Israeli settlements, for example, then said to the Palestinians 'I got Israel to stop new settlements' and moved forward toward Middle Eastern peace.

Instead the self-proclaimed Great Deal Maker got nothing in return for giving up this huge bargaining chip.

Moron!

Third, he abruptly announced a US troop pullout from Syria, leaving an ally, the Kurds, exposed and creating a power vacuum. Only two weeks (2 weeks!) later, the Russian and Turkish foreign ministers met to arrange the post-US regional power allocation.

Both have learned how to achieve their strategic objectives: simply praise Trump to his face then wait for a rash decision in their favor.

Moron!

Fourth, he demanded that the Federal Reserve Bank Chairman Jerome Powell not raise interest rates in December 2018. That forced Powell to raise rates even if he didn't want to, just to avoid looking like a Trump stooge and lowering his and the Bank's credibility with markets.

Moron!

Fifth, he reneged on a stop-gap funding agreement with Congress last Christmas, simply because some right wing zealots spoke out, resulting in a partial government shut down.

Imagine what international political and business leaders think of an American president who publicly backtracks – overnight and to the detriment of his own economy! - when Ann Coulter says so.

Moron!

I could go on.

But the best example was Trump's decision to run for President in the first place.

Only a moron would run for the President with so many skeletons in his closet. Things like operating a fraudulent charity, which New York State has already closed down with more prosecutions to follow.

Or secretly paying off sex partners under a false name. Did he really think the news media would ignore that one?

Or money laundering and related financial crimes (I'm going out on a limb here, but not a very big one) in his real estate businesses. Did he really think publicity seeking state and federal prosecutors would miss all that?

Or holding nutty beliefs, like that he knows more about war than generals. Really? From sound bites on Fox News?

Tillerson was right. Trump really is a moron.

I fear where this all leads.

What I Learned About the US Senate in Alaska

I visited Alaska last summer with my wife and learned something unsettling about US Senate and Electoral College voting patterns there.

Alaska's huge but, it turns out, almost no one lives there. Its total population, about 740,000 people, equals Joe Kennedy's congressional district, i.e. ours.

But Alaska sends 2 Senators to Washington, each theoretically representing about 370,000 people, i.e. half the state's population. Compare that to Elizabeth Warren and Ed Markey, our two Senators, each representing about 3.5 million Mass residents, i.e. half of our population.

Alaskans get more D.C. power per person than we do!

Now consider that over half their population lives in greater Anchorage, making Anchorage a city-state for electoral purposes.

What happens in Anchorage reverberates in Washington DC.

Let's expand on this to other states.

The 20 smallest states – Iowa, Nevada, Arkansas, Mississippi, Kansas, New Mexico, Nebraska, West Virginia, Idaho, Hawaii, New Hampshire, Maine, Montana, Rhode Island, Delaware, South Dakota, North Dakota, Alaska, Vermont and Wyoming – average about 1.7 million people per US Senator.

But the 15 largest states – California, Texas, Florida, New York, Pennsylvania, Illinois, Ohio, Georgia, North Carolina, Michigan, New Jersey, Virginia, Washington, Arizona and Massachusetts – average about 6.5 million people per US Senator.

In round numbers, the 40 Senators from the small states represent 20% of the US population while the 30 from the large states represent 60%.

Now consider their voting patterns.

Thirteen of the 20 smallest states are reliably Republican meaning 26 Senators in DC.

Eight of the 15 largest are reliably Democratic sending 16 Senators to DC.

This Constitutionally gerrymandered situation has at least 3 political implications.

First, Republicans are structurally more than half way to passing – or blocking - any Senate legislation while representing only a very small, largely rural, largely white population.

Meanwhile we, as a country, are increasingly urban and non-white.

Second, the Electoral College, the body that actually elects the US President based on the number of Senators and House seats per state, far overrepresents each small state voter.

It's not '1 man or woman, 1 vote' for President but closer to '1 man or woman in Alaska, 1 vote, but 1 man or woman in Massachusetts, 0.1 votes'.

Third, this bodes badly for domestic tranquility, the reason Madison and his buddies wrote the Constitution in the first place. Popular vote winners but Electoral College losers will, I suspect, get fed up after another round or two.

We've already seen it twice since 2000, W. Bush and Trump. How long will a US majority succumb to minority rule in the Senate and Presidency?

My take away from Alaska: we're getting onto thin ice (get it? Alaska!) politically with an energized Left in the racially diverse, urbanized large states and Right in the white, rural small ones.

I don't know how long before that thin ice cracks.

Chain Migration and Public Education Funding

I recently had brunch with several friends, all mid-60s, all third generation Americans, all comfortably middle class.

And all beneficiaries of both chain migration and excellent public education.

The background stories were remarkably similar, varying only in specifics.

One fellow, a successful attorney, told of his grandfather who emigrated here from Ukraine in the early 1900s then brought his brothers over, one at a time. All my friend's siblings are prosperous professionals today.

Another's grandfather settled in a hardscrabble New England town and achieved only very modest economic success himself. His two children, though, did well in public school and college: one became a doctor, the other a lawyer.

Another's grandparents settled in upstate New York and were dirt poor – literally – most of their lives. 'Dirt poor' from farming, mainly vegetables and chickens. They had arrived courtesy of older siblings and avoided starving during the Great Depression by eating their own crops.

Fast forward two generations: one grandchild holds a law degree from Boston College, another a public administration degree from Harvard, a third is a senior hospital administrator and a fourth runs a multi-million dollar family business.

The common theme: the children of these poor immigrants received excellent education at the local public schools and went on to prosper.

And the grandchildren – my generation – is the solid middle class that so defines America.

But, also over brunch, my friends and I discussed another theme, discrimination. All our grandparents were looked down on by society. They were mocked for their accents, customs or religions. They took the worst jobs, those that 'normal' Americans didn't want like my great uncle, a New York City sky scrapper window washer who spent his entire career outdoors, 30+ stories high.

As I listened to those stories, and there were many more, I thought about our current immigrants' lives. Similar discrimination, possibly even more.

But less compensating educational and related support especially in the inner cities due largely to underfunded, low quality public schools.

This strikes me as a shockingly poor national investment.

I saw the result of our historical public education investment sitting around the brunch table. I'd guess that each couple – a fairly representative group of Easton and Mansfield residents - has paid over $1 million in state and federal taxes over their lifetimes.

(That math, in case you want to check: $100,000+ family income for 30+ years at a 33% effective tax rate.)

That's a pretty good return on the investment our country made in immigrants two generations ago.

Will we do the same today?

I worry that if we continue to underfund public education in the name of the middle class tax cuts perpetually sponsored by Republicans, we'll create a permanent underclass of underachieving, needy folks.

The recent Boston Globe series on urban valedictorians underscores that problem.

But if all the currently-demonized immigrant kids get a solid public education, social supports, attend college and develop as our parents and we did, then our country's future looks remarkably good.

To invest in the future or not. That, it seems to me, is the core immigration question we consistently fail to address.

On Student Debt

I'm a huge fan of higher education.

I'm an equally huge opponent of debt based education financing for at least three reasons:

First, debt reduces students' abilities to change majors as they advance in college, especially if the change adds more time – meaning debt – to their education.

Second, debt forces people to take higher paying jobs upon graduation, eliminating potentially impactful growth opportunities like internships, social service positions, travel, Peace Corps and similar.

Third, debt inhibits normal financial and personal development like buying new cars or houses, starting a business or taking career risks.

Instead of debt financing, I favor tuition free public colleges and universities for in-state students.

I'd even go one step further and provide monthly stipends to cover basic expenses – room, board, transportation and fees - during students' 3 year (!) undergraduate period.

I've seen this system in action. Indeed, I got my BA in it, at Lancaster University in northern England.

The system worked wonderfully.

My English peers received, in addition to free tuition, need-based monthly stipends from the government. The wealthiest got at least something and the poorest, those without parental economic assistance, received enough to get by, albeit living frugally.

My friends felt both entitled to all this largesse – they had earned good grades after all, and their parents paid taxes – and grateful. This was their one chance, they realized, to get a free, high quality college education.

My college graduation rate was well over 90%.

How well did my 3-year English bachelor's degree compare to a 4-year American? It served me perfectly well in a US master's program a few years later.

Can we afford this? Of course! Many countries do today. The English have for years, based on three guiding principles:

First, they standardized on a 3-year bachelor's degree.

Second, they only admitted college-ready students. The English traditionally encouraged high school graduates to take time off – sometimes years – to gain work experience and begin college only when ready.

Indeed, they paid 'mature students', those over 24, more.

And third, they chose to invest in their population's education.

Compare that to our recent tax cuts and consider the impact on former Senator Bob Corker of Tennessee according to the Boston Globe's analysis.

Corker, apparently a savvy real estate investor who voted for the tax cuts, saved $1 million on his personal taxes.

That same $1 million could have funded 400+ college students for a year and, presumably, increased the graduation rate.

Expand this example nationally.

Students graduating with no debt will put $100+ billion annually into our consumption based economy – that's the 45 million people each currently paying $300/month in college loan debt service - thus stimulating overall economic growth.

Huge positive economic impacts for us all.

Now imagine if a beneficiary of that system was you or your child.

I've seen this work.

I hope someday we'll have it here.

Economic Consequences

There are at least 2 consequences of any economic activity: the intended goal and the side effects.

Consider a simple case, a summer drive into Boston. The intended goal is getting there comfortably, safely and quickly.

The side effects include air pollution.

The private sector, by and large, focuses on intended goals and, in this example, builds increasingly reliable cars, remarkably inexpensively by historical standards.

The government, by contrast, focuses more on side effects with increasingly stringent regulations that restrict car exhaust for example.

The differing private and public foci help define our two political parties. Republicans typically focus on economic efficiency, i.e. generating the intended goals less expensively; Democrats, typically, the opposite.

Both parties fudge. Republicans minimize the negative side effects and Democrats minimize efficiency losses from regulations.

Now consider coal fired electricity plant pollution standards, a current national issue.

The Trump administration recently proposed increasing the allowable carbon dioxide emissions from 1400 pounds per megawatt hour to 1900.

They praise the intended goals – energy independence, cheaper electricity and jobs in West Virginia – and downplay the medical sides effects, admitting to 'only' an increase of 1000 additional annual deaths by 2030.

Yes, the Trump administration estimates this.

Outraged Democrats respond that the loosened regs will cause 40% more deaths than Trump's estimate, plus up to 15,000 annual new cases of heart and lung disease, a rise in bronchitis, tens of thousands of missed school days and higher healthcare spending.

Scarcely a mention of energy independence or West Virginia jobs.

For Republicans, the (maximized) intended goals far outweigh the (minimized) negative side effects.

For Democrats, the (maximized) negative side effects outweigh the (minimized) intended goals.

Rather than admit this and use reliable and agreed upon analytics, both parties play to their semi-rational bases.

Republicans rail against all regulations claiming 'economic catastrophe looms.'

Democrats rail against all *de*regulation claiming 'human catastrophe looms.'

We, the people, get mediocre governance.

Ponder that next time you drive into Boston in the summer, presumably in a very reliable, air-conditioned car with the windows closed.

After all, it's increasingly hot outside due to global warming and sometimes the polluted air smells bad.

Why Inequality Should Matter to You

(Apologies in advance for the wonkiness of this column.)

We generally overlook, in discussions of taxes and government spending, the health impacts of economic inequality.

These are not only big but, In my opinion, overwhelming.

Inequality affects our health in two main ways.

First, the lower your economic status, the higher your disease rates and lower your life expectancy. Many studies have documented this.

Imagine two people with *identical* cholesterol, blood pressure, blood sugar, smoking status and BMI. The lower economic status one faces higher disease rates and a shorter life expectancy than the higher status person with gradations:

- People in the top 5% - that's households earning over $240,000 – live the longest on average
- People in the top quarter – households over $130,000 – live a bit less long, again on average
- People in the next quarter – over $80,000 – even less long
- People in the next quarter – over $50,000 – shorter still, etc.

The New England Journal of Medicine put it this way: "there is something about low socio-economic status itself that increases the risk of premature death".

I'd actually argue, based on my own research, that low economic status is probably a bigger medical risk than moderately high cholesterol, blood pressure, blood sugar or BMI.

Second, the amount of economic inequality is a risk factor.

Put simply, the greater the inequality in a country, the higher the disease rates and lower the life expectancies of *all* socio-economic groups compared to a norm.

High economic status Americans live, in other words, on average, longer than low economic status Americans but less long than similarly high status folks from more equal societies, notably western Europe and Japan.

Again, documented in the medical literature.

Let's apply these two factors – high economic inequality and mortality gradations by income – to the recent American experience.

From 2012 – 2017, the amount of US wealth owned by the richest 1% of Americans grew substantially; they ended up owning slightly more than the bottom 90% of us. That's pretty unequal.

Over the same time period, the US GDP grew by 20%, US health spending grew by 20% and US average life expectancies *fell* by about .15 years.

More economic growth led to more inequality. Increased medical spending didn't overcome the negative health impacts.

Though we far outspend any other country on medical care, we have a relatively low number of centenarians: 22 per 100,000 Americans, compared to 54 per 100,000 Japanese, 32 French, 32 Italians and 39 Portuguese.

When next you consider tax policy, government spending and social programs, think about the health impacts on yourself and the rest of us.

You may find it a life-or-death decision.

Cruelty as Public Policy

We've gone, I fear, from being Ronald Reagan's shining light on a hill to a country exalting in cruelty to the poor and unfortunate.

Two recent examples.

First, President Trump fired Homeland Security Secretary Kirstjen Nielsen for being insufficiently tough on immigrants seeking asylum.

Her primary offense was ending child separations at the border, in part at least because of a federal judge's order.

The law, in other words.

That excuse – 'it's illegal' – didn't impress Trump, and the subsequent too-gentle policy of holding immigrants in cells for months proved too kind to Trump and his chief immigration lieutenant, Stephen 'We-should-not-allow-poor-immigrants-who-don't-speak-English-to-come-here-even-though-my-great-grandmother-arrived-here-speaking-only-Yiddish' Miller.

They want more illegal child separations, mirroring Barry Goldwater's infamous moral dictate that "extremism in defense of liberty is no vice. And the pursuit of justice is no virtue." (Yes, Goldwater, a leading Republican for decades, actually said that. I'm not making this stuff up.)

I'd hate to see a real vice if child separation isn't one.

Second, Secretary of Health and Human Services Alex Azar, speaking in Boston last month decried Medicaid for insuring able bodied males.

Suspend disbelief temporarily.

About 60% of Medicaid recipients already work.

Another 30% suffer from mental health issues or addictions like schizophrenia or opioid addiction.

Apparently Azar wants to withhold health coverage from sick poor people, presumably to score political points because the economics don't stand up.

Cruelty sells among Republicans, not wisdom or compassion.

One non-cruel way to reduce Medicaid costs, if Republicans actually wanted that, is to raise the minimum wage and provide job skill training.

But no, rather than help folks in need – and the Medicaid income cut-off of $18,000 a year certainly qualifies as 'in need' - the Trumpees block minimum wage increases, cut training programs and assume ('pray', 'hope', 'scream') that tax cuts for job creators, a.k.a. the rich, will solve the problem.

It never has, but understanding history or economics was never a Republican strong point.

Why Republicans choose cruelty over compassion and punishment over investment as public policies escapes me.

But they certainly have.

What a world.

Thoughts on July 4

Independence Day reminds us of Thomas Jefferson's stirring 1776 Declaration of Independence.

The Declaration consists of 2 distinct parts: the famous Preamble that sets out Jefferson's view of government and the specific indictments against King George III.

Let me quote and highlight some of the Preamble's soaring prose:

We hold these truths to be **self-evident**, that all men are created **equal**, that they are endowed by their Creator with certain **unalienable Rights**, that among these are **Life, Liberty and the pursuit of Happiness.**

That **to secure these rights, Governments are instituted** among Men, deriving their just powers from the consent of the governed.

That **whenever any Form of Government becomes destructive of these ends**, it is the Right of the People to **alter or to abolish it** and to institute new Government, laying its foundation on such principles and organizing its powers in such form, as to them shall seem **most likely to effect their Safety and Happiness**.

The government, in brief, exists to secure equality of Life, Liberty and Happiness for the People it serves.

How well have we succeeded over the past 243 years? Some indicators:

- The richest 1% of Americans own about 40% of the total wealth in our country, or about as much wealth as the poorest 90%.
- Our wealth distribution is more unequal than at any point since 1962.
- The lowest income Americans live about 12 years less long than the highest income Americans.

- African Americans are about 5x more likely to get incarcerated than white Americans.
- The average woman's unadjusted annual salary is about 20% lower than the average male's.
- The average African American male earned about 35% less than the average white American male.

Not a stellar grade on Jefferson's equality scale.

Now consider some specific charges against King George III's 'repeated injuries and usurpations' in Jefferson's indictment, each alongside a current administration example. I'll limit this to 5:

King George refused his Assent to Laws necessary for the public good.

- Donald Trump has rolled back environmental protection laws that will cause, according to his own EPA estimates, 1000+ annual deaths.

King George cut off Trade with all parts of the world.

- Donald Trump has imposed trade obstacles with many parts of the world.

King George has excited domestic insurrections.

- Donald Trump has encouraged violence against his opponents, as in his campaign statement to supporters about protesters: "knock the crap out of them, would you?"

King George refused to encourage migration to the Colonies.

- Donald Trump wants to build a wall to keep immigrants out.

King George has obstructed the Administration of Justice (though he was never charged or convicted).

- The Mueller Report detailed 10 separate instances of Donald Trump's obstruction of justice.

I'm not sure Thomas Jefferson and his co-authors Ben Franklin and John Adams would be entirely pleased with our progress since 1776.

So enjoy the Independence Day vacation and rest up...

We have a lot of work still ahead of us.

Gary Fradin

A Future of Hope or Fear:
What Campaign Contribution Patterns Tell Us

Americans donate money to political campaigns for one of two main reasons: hope or fear about the future. Over the past couple of decades, we've seen a remarkable shift in campaign funding sources between the Republicans and Democrats.

Historically, the richest Americans donated primarily to Republican candidates, with 68% of Forbes 400 members, for example, donating to Republicans in the 1981 – 82 election cycle.

This decreased to only 59% by the 2011 – 2012 cycle.

During that time period, membership in the Forbes 400 shifted dramatically from manufacturing and energy production (gas and oil) to knowledge and technology companies.

Specifically, 89 of the 1981 members (22%) made their money in oil, compared to only 14 in 2011 (3.5%). Today's Forbes Top 10 include Jeff Bezos, Larry Paige and Larry Ellison, founders of Amazon, Google and Oracle, companies unimagined in 1981, all Democratic donors.

While the very wealthy shift donations from Republicans and Democrats, small donors do the opposite. President Trump is set to break Barak Obama's record for campaign contributions of less than $200.

Why would wealthy knowledge and technology folks donate to Democrats while middle class Americans switch to Republicans?

The answer, I suggest, is differing views of the future.

Business entrepreneurs are forward looking optimists who donate to campaigns that will help their companies and business sectors grow.

They want higher investments in education to create more knowledge workers and consumers, more investment in recent immigrants who will produce and use their products and higher taxes on very wealthy people to fund social programs.

Increasingly, they see Democratic candidates as agents of this dynamic, growth oriented, hopeful future.

Middle class Americans today, though, tend to worry about the future and donate to campaigns that offer to protect them from it. Differently from business entrepreneurs, they see the future as threatening, with stagnant wages, job competition from foreigners and foreign trade deals that harm them.

They want lower taxes so they can keep more of their (relatively shrinking) wages.

Increasingly, they see Republican candidates as agents of protection against this grim future, candidates who will turn back the clock and, in a slogan, 'Make American Great Again'.

Is the future one of hope or fear? Is the glass half full and filling or half empty and emptying?

The way you answer those questions suggests, based on campaign contribution trends at least, how you lean politically.

How to save $27 million in local taxes

Easton faces a stark tax choice over the next couple of months: we have to choose whether to spend $59 million or $86 million on our local elementary schools.

A new elementary school will cost Easton taxpayers $59 million plus interest, with payments spread over 30 years. The Massachusetts School Building Authority has offered to fund the additional construction cost but gives us only until November to accept their offer.

On the other hand, repairing our existing schools will cost Easton taxpayers $86 million – current estimate, current dollars plus interest - with payments on an as-needed basis over the next 15 – 30 years. No Mass School Building Authority subsidy.

The new school saves Easton taxpayers $27 million.

Some background: Easton applied to the state competitive school grant program in 2011 and then reapplied every year since.

In 2017, our application was accepted for consideration. That started a lengthy process including a needs and feasibility study, evaluation of about a dozen different construction options, development of a detailed education program and a design study.

That lengthy process of working with the design firm plus the back-and-forth with the Building Authority generated the most appropriate design to address Easton's educational needs at the lowest feasible cost.

The Building Authority approved Easton's submission this summer.

The money is now available and we have to vote on it. It's a take-it-now-or-start-all-over-again vote; there's no 'let's make some changes and vote again' option.

If we vote no, some other community will get the money and we'll start the entire process all over again, just like in 2011. It will take years, perhaps a decade or more, for similar state funding to become available to us again.

During that time, our school repair costs will continue and new construction costs will rise.

The likely result: our schools will need to cut programs and staff to fund boiler replacement, asbestos removal, ADA compliance and all the rest.

Cut programs or raise taxes. Probably both. Where else does $86 million come from?

As an Easton home owner and property tax payer, I know which option I prefer. Finance a new school sensibly over 30 years, save $27 million and maintain our existing school quality and programs.

It's as close to a no-brainer as exists.

Why Medicare for All Must Pass

I'm not a huge Medicare fan for a bunch of reasons including:

- Too many coverage gaps, like no dental
- Too confusing, with over half of Medicare beneficiaries unsure about their options according to surveys
- Too expensive, with premiums, deductibles and supplements often running $5000 per person annually *or more*
- Too paternalistic, with physicians penalized for not providing tests that independent research has shown to be non-beneficial or harmful (e.g. annual mammograms and psa)
- Too restrictive, with old technologies often required, like 1990s era kidney dialysis
- Too influenced by lobbyists, with beneficiaries unable to save themselves or the system money with less expensive / similar quality care overseas.

With all these problems – and more - why do I see passage of Medicare for All as so critical?

The answer is political and historical, not economic or medical. The US government, in my opinion, needs to show Americans that it can function and provide at least some important services to us.

We've had a 40+ year experience of shifting service provision from the public to private sectors. The old tax-and-spend liberals have been soundly defeated by the cut-taxes-and-let-the-private-sector-do-it team, from Ronald Reagan to 'read my lips, no new taxes' Bush 41 to 'the era of big government is over' Bill Clinton and beyond.

As a consequence, we face today crumbling infrastructure, dystopian traffic congestion, huge income inequality, lousy inner city schools, an increasingly polluted environment, 3rd world quality public transportation and a mind boggling complicated, inefficient and expensive healthcare system that currently consumes about 18% of our GDP, double most other developed countries.

The government's track record of wins on the domestic front is pretty weak. Obamacare – the last nationally impactful social legislation - reduced the number of medically uninsured by millions, but that program has been gutted by Trump.

What else has the government done to improve our lives since 2000 that it didn't do prior? What major domestic problems has it addressed at all, let alone successfully…gun control? Economic inequality? Climate change? Traffic congestion? Obesity?

I can't think of any despite trillions in government revenues.

As a result, our population has turned increasingly skeptical. Public trust in our government fell from about 80% in the tax-and-spend 1960s to 20% in the don't-tax-or-spend atmosphere today.

That's unhealthy for our democracy and our county. The federal government surely should do *something* besides be its current dysfunctional self.

That's where Medicare for All comes in. The government can expand our existing Medicare program – problematic though it is – from the current 60 million beneficiaries to all 320 million of us fairly easily. (Nothing is easy in healthcare.) The infrastructure exists at both the care provision and financial levels and Medicare currently gets high satisfaction ratings from beneficiaries.

We can do all this relatively quickly, faster than building new roads or railroads and more visibly than cleaning the environment or reducing economic inequality.

Will Medicare for All save us money? I suspect so, especially over time though reduced administrative overhead, currently about 25% of premium, combined carriers and providers.

Will it expand medical coverage? Probably, just as Medicare has for the elderly.

Will it improve our national health metrics? Again probably over time, as people stop self rationing medical care due to current high deductibles, often $2500 or more.

Will it solve all of our healthcare problems? No.

I don't love Medicare. But I love this country and I think our government badly needs a win.

Medicare for All seems to me the best way to regain public trust in government, at least in the short term.

That's why I see passing it as so critical.

Gary Fradin

The Real Cost of Reducing Environmental Protections

Economists and the courts sometimes assign economic values to life and death. Though perhaps unsavory to some, this exercise can provide a useful way to evaluate public policies.

Consider the trade-offs we face in product safety regulations. Raising safety requirements may mean fewer jobs and the reverse; reducing safety requirements to create more jobs may lead to higher death rates.

At what point are products 'safe enough' and job growth 'strong enough'?

Consider the Trump administration's 2017 overhaul of federal restrictions on coal burning power plants to create more jobs. The resulting air pollution, the EPA estimated in 2018, will cause 1000 – 1400 deaths annually by 2030.

Did the Administration generate enough jobs to justify this mortality increase?

On the harm side, we know that about 1200 additional annual deaths will result. That's the midpoint between the EPAs' 1000 – 1400 estimate.

On the benefit side, WSAZ, a Charleston, West Virginia TV station, calculated the number of new coal jobs that resulted through March, 2019 in West Virginia and Kentucky: 1991. Each pays, according to ABC News and Money Magazine, around $70,000. For the sake of this discussion, assume that this trend continues.

The economic gain estimate: 2000 jobs at $70K = $140,000,000 per year.

$140 million divided by 1200 annual deaths = $116,667 per life.

Is that good or bad?

One way to answer is to compare the $116,667 value of each life shortened from air pollution to victim payouts from other disasters – say from the September 11th Victim Compensation Fund, established after the 9/11 terrorist bombings - on the assumption that each American's life should be about equally valuable.

That average payout was $2,082,128 in 2003 dollars or, inflation adjusted, about $2,747.323 today, roughly 23x the value of each life shortened by air pollution.

Did the Administration create enough new coal jobs to justify the higher death rates?

The answer, based on this analysis, appears to be no.

Not by a mile.

The Hypocrisy of Power

Consider the evolution of two leading Republican statesmen's thinking, Secretary of State Mike Pompeo and Senator Lindsay Graham, as they gained political power.

And consider why political ascendancy leads to such blatant hypocrisy.

Perhaps Seinfeld's George Costanza was right when he observed that it's not a lie if you believe it when you say it.

First, Pompeo, clearly intellectually gifted - 1st in his class at West Point and editor of the Harvard Law Review – spent 6 years in Congress including on the House Select Committee on Benghazi prior to joining the Trump administration.

He then said the Obama administration's response to Congressional inquiries was "deeply obstructive of getting the American people the facts that they needed."

His co-authored addendum to the Committee's report called the Obama administration "more concerned with politics and Secretary Clinton's legacy than with its people in Benghazi" and "so focused on the next election that it lost sight of its duty to tell the American people the truth".

That was then.

Now he calls Congressional inquisitors into Ukrainian misdeeds 'bullies' and 'intimidators', apparently unconcerned that the American people may not get the facts they need or that the Trump administration has lost sight of its duty to tell the American people the truth.

In other words, exactly what he accused the Obama administration of doing.

"I will use all means at my disposal to prevent and expose any attempts to intimidate the dedicated professionals" in the State Department he stated.

Odd phrase for a former Benghazi intimidator.

Second, Senator Lindsay Graham, a brilliantly articulate 25-year veteran of Congress, has enjoyed a similarly hypocritical intellectual development.

His 1999 prosecution of Bill Clinton helped define modern impeachment. A President could lose his job, he stated, if "your conduct as a public official is clearly out of bounds."

"Impeachment is not about punishment. Impeachment is about cleansing the office. Impeachment is about restoring honor and integrity to the office."

Works for me.

But it apparently no longer works for Graham unless he sees Donald Trump as a paragon of honor and integrity.

Trump is many things of which honor and integrity are not two.

Neither Pompeo or Graham strike me as particularly unscrupulous or odious. Rather they seem like normal politicians, ready to claim the high moral ground when it suits them then change positions when their responsibilities or poll numbers shift.

And always ready to accuse their opponents of flip flopping.

That all this seems normal upsets me. I'd prefer to see our political leaders as people of integrity and our voters as good judges of character. I would hope that we would be led by men and women of honor.

Instead, we're led by the unscrupulous, the vindictive, the win-at-any-cost group that cares only about gaining and holding power but not how to use that power for the greater good.

'It's not a lie if you believe it at the time'. George Costanza got a laugh when he said it on TV.

Today we give a frustrated, gallows humor type sigh of acquiesce when politicians practice what Costanza preached.

Thoughts After a Long Walk Through Easton

I walked 8 miles through Easton last Saturday afternoon including circuits of North Easton Village, Frothingham Park and the school fields.

A beautiful afternoon outing.

But exhausting!

My first thought the next morning: 'too much, you overdid it yesterday'.

Second thought, still while attempting to negotiate fatigued legs: 'those Central American migrants do this day-after-day, in uncomfortable heat, often barefoot.'

Followed immediately by 'they must really want to leave their home countries and come here'

And 'I want people that tough, determined and committed to come here.'

Then 'if we provide good education, integration supports and skill training, they'll accomplish great stuff.'

Finally, because I'm admittedly somewhat odd, lines from Emma Lazarus' famous sonnet at the Statue of Liberty that I ultimately had to look up:

Give me your tired, your poor, your huddled masses yearning to breathe free

The wretched refuse of your teaming shore.

Send them, the homeless, tempest-tossed to me.

I began thinking in poorly imitated Lazarus' stanzas while waiting for my morning coffee:

How far we've fallen from when we were great enough to welcome impoverished foreigners.

How far we've fallen to put into cages the people who risk everything to come here.

How far we've fallen to cut immigration supports and skill training for the tired and poor, yearning to breathe free.

How far we've fallen to send the wretched refuse away at the point of a gun.

How far we've fallen to call homeless, tempest-tossed folks 'animals, not people'.

How far we've fallen in the eyes of the world and of our future generations.

How far we've fallen according to our national moral compass.

Thoroughly depressed, I drank my morning coffee, made interestingly, exclusively from Latin American beans. Yes, I looked that up.

How far we've fallen.

Socialist Threats to America

Don't expect a frontal assault from the socialist forces that threaten our liberty.

Expect instead small, insidious steps, the far more typical socialist playbook.

Beware especially of attractive sounding programs aimed at the elderly and children, socialists' favorite targets.

Consider healthcare.

The great Ronald Reagan presciently warned in the early 1960s: "One of the traditional methods of imposing socialism on a people has been by way of medicine." Reagan knew his stuff.

From the healthcare base, he continued 'it's a short step to all the rest of socialism'.

Where do we see socialized medicine in America? President George H. W. Bush told us years ago: Medicare. He called it 'socialized medicine'.

Such insight.

'Write your Congressman', Reagan admonished during the initial Medicare debate, 'Tell him you don't want socialized medicine!'

Our failure to follow his advice has cost us dearly.

Today 45 million Americans have Medicare and about 80% like the program.

See how well the socialists have done their job? They've brainwashed our senior citizens!

Elderly Americans can no longer differentiate right from wrong, patriotism from socialism.

But it's not too late. Follow Reagan's advice today.

Disenroll in Medicare! Cancel your colonoscopy! Be a patriot!

But healthcare was just the beginning. Consider the next step, socialism's corruption of our youth.

No, not through socialist free K - 12 public education like in Russia, North Korea or China.

But the National Football League.

The NFL shares its $5 billion TV revenue equally among all teams. Winners don't get more for winning or losers less for losing.

Sounds to me like a glorified Soviet socialist collective. 'From each according to their abilities' ... the Patriots win more than the Raiders .... 'to each according to their needs' .... the Raiders need a new stadium.

Art Model, owner of the original Cleveland Browns, called NFL owners 'fat-cat Republicans who vote socialist on football.'

Why win?

In fact economists estimate that winning 10% more football games generates only about 0.14% more revenue, about 1 tenth of 1%.

Winning doesn't pay. Losing doesn't hurt. The socialist NFL has seen to that.

What lesson does that teach our youth?

More insidiously, the salary cap means really good players – the hard workers who achieve athletic excellence, the ones our children should idolize like the Pats' Trey Flowers, a 4th round draft pick who became a star – leave the team in their prime for cost reasons.

How do we tell our children, the ones, wearing Trey Flowers jerseys, that the Soviet-style NFL collective won't allow good players to stay?

I worry about how this corrupts our youth.

The NFL teaches sharing and socialism, not winning and patriotism.

Boycott the socialist NFL!

Boycott Medicare!

Follow Ronald Reagan's advice: Tell your Congressman that stool softeners lead to socialism, Diovan to dictatorship and collective sports bargaining to collectives.

A complete socialist takeover might be just around the corner.

Gary Fradin

2020

What the Democrats Get Wrong About Impeachment

The Democrats mistakenly think impeachment is about Constitutional violations and the associated remedies. They mistakenly think it's a legal process. That's why they focus on facts, testimony, witnesses and Constitutional law.

None of those are relevant to today's impeachment process.

Instead, impeachment today is about television ratings; it's a made-for-TV event, not a political or legal exercise. The goal of today's impeachment proceeding is to get eyeballs onto TV screens and reinforce tribalism, not to promulgate a compelling legal case.

The Republicans get it. Impeachment is about television.

Consider Trump's attorneys. They're the FOX TV All Star Legal Talking Heads Team.

Take Ken Starr an articulate jurist whose historical legacy is a 4 year (four year!) investigation into Bill Clinton's sex life. Yech. I'm not sure which is sleazier: Clinton's sex life or the investigators who spent 4 years (four years!) studying and documenting it.

Sex sleaze got eyeballs onto TV screens then and Starr a regular gig on Fox now so he's qualified as an impeachment defense attorney. Yech again.

Then there's Alan Dershowitz, Harvard Law School's great criminal defense expert who argues impeachment constitutional issues.

Dershowitz is not a constitutional lawyer. He has published, according to Lawrence Tribe, Harvard's *actual* constitutional expert, no (i.e. zero) scholarly books or articles about constitutional law. "He doesn't bring any relevant knowledge, as far as I know" said Tribe, a long time Harvard colleague.

Hiring Dershowitz to argue impeachment constitutional law is like having a urologist deliver your baby. A vaguely related specialty with some knowledge overlap with obstetrics, but a poor choice if you're interested in maternal and infant health.

Dershowitz is articulate, a TV ratings machine and perceived defender of the President so he fits the profile.

I have a bone to pick with Dershowitz on his client choices. According to the excellent 1990 film Reversal of Fortune based on his own book: "I take cases because I get pissed off" (direct Dershowitz quote) meaning he gets angry that the government oversteps its power when prosecuting unempowered folks.

Think of a poor, badly educated kid being prosecuted for murder based on flimsy evidence.

I admired his sentiments then. They stirred my pride in the American legal system.

But Donald Trump isn't an unempowered, poor victim of overzealous government prosecutors. He runs the executive branch of the US government!

Instead, Trump's the thug who publicly accused poor kids of the Central Park jogger murder in the 1980s, didn't rent to minorities in the 1970s and admires the fine white nationalists who chanted 'Jews will not replace us' in Charlotte a couple years ago.

Trump offers Dershowitz something more valuable than integrity: an hour on national TV, speaking in the US Senate chamber with all 100 US Senators forced to listen.

So Dershowitz takes the job and Trump's base gets exciting TV from a non-expert.

Trump – like Dershowitz, Starr, the White House and Fox News – knows that incisive legal arguments, detailed factual descriptions and complex Constitutional analyses bore people.

The foolish Democrats miss this and aim to get impeachment facts and law right instead.

They don't have a chance.

Political Definitions Today

Words used to mean something. That allowed us all to engage in useful political dialogue.

Consider some words we currently use, then ask yourself if they mean anything at all these days.

Main Stream Media – a pejorative term for news organizations that don't spout right wing talking points and therefore practice 'dishonesty, total deceit and deception'. (Trump quote) The Main Stream Media includes the New York Times, CNN and CBS among others but not Fox News.

Interestingly the New York Times has won 117 Pulitzer Prizes for journalistic excellence, CNN has won 21 Peabody Awards for enlightening and invigorating television reporting, CBS has won 24 Peabody's for 60 Minutes alone and Fox hasn't won any.

This confirms that the Main Stream Media is a massive conspiracy (see below), aimed at destroying America as we know it.

Fair and Balanced – the opposite of Main Stream Media and housed primarily at Fox News, the voice of conservative politics according to its founder Roger Ailes. In today's lexicon, 'fair' means biased and 'balanced' means parochial.

Interestingly Fox dropped this moniker in 2017 due to Ailes' public downfall though, according to the Main Stream Media, nothing has changed editorially, meaning it's still fair and balanced.

Or biased and parochial. Take your pick. They mean the same thing.

Conspiracies – the unscrupulous, nefarious, unethical, underhanded and borderline illegal methods used by loathsome, devious and immoral people, typically uncovered by fair and balanced reporters.

An example: "the Democrat's conspiracy to overthrow the president knows no shame" from Sonoran News, the Conservative Voice of Arizona which continues, "Democrats need to keep their constituency in the dark…They do not care about your country."

Interestingly the Main Stream Media indulges in far fewer conspiracy theories suggesting, to the fair and balanced media, a massive coverup of the evil deeds they see behind liberal politician.

And, presumably, also behind each Pulitzer and Peabody Prize award.

Governing Philosophy and **Hypocrisy** – two words with virtually identical meanings depending on whether your favored party is in power or not.

Take the Republican Senate leadership's principled refusal to vote on Merrick Garland for a Supreme Court vacancy in 2016 because a (Democratic) president shouldn't appoint Supreme Court justices just prior to an election. 'The American people need to speak on this' summarized Mitch McConnell.

Then, under a Republican President, McConnell said that, if a Supreme Court vacancy occurs just prior to the 2020 election, 'we'd fill it.'

Or the ever eloquent Senator Lindsay Graham on impeachment witnesses in 1999 as a Republican Trial Manager: witnesses uncover "the truth, the whole truth, and nothing but the truth" and are therefore essential.

But not today: "I don't really need to hear a lot of witnesses" despite news reports of critical information not included in the Trump impeachment, a.k.a. 'the whole truth'.

Or federal deficits, the most important economic issue vocalized by (out of power) Republicans during the Obama years. Those same deficits, now approaching a trillion dollars a year under Trump, elicit nary a peep.

Whataboutism – a strange term that means admitting to accusatory facts, then saying the other guy does it too so it's not really that bad, as in 'what about the Democrats?'

My mother, and probably yours too, destroyed this notion while raising children: 'just because the other kid lies doesn't mean you should too.' Surely our civic leaders should have standards slightly higher than those of pre-adolescent kids.

But they don't. Fox in their fair and balanced presentation regularly ridicules Democrats who point out Republican foibles with whataboutisms.

Then conveniently ignore the underlying accusations.

Bipartisan – a meaningless term superseded by a Vince Lombardism.

Bipartisan used to mean sharing a vision as in 'Republicans and Democrats share certain fundamental values.'

Today bipartisan means 'I want you to agree with my point of view' as in 'if I compromise with you, I will get primaried by someone even more extreme'. Vince summarized today's bipartisanism with his famous saying that 'winning isn't everything; it's the only thing.'

In summary: Our fair and balanced news media regularly reports evil conspiracies. When challenged on the facts by the Main Stream Media, they respond with whataboutisms that mask a Lombardisque approach to public leadership.

Oh, what Merriam-Webster would say …

If anyone consulted them anymore.

Gary Fradin

Compare, Contrast and Excuses

Let's compare Trump's bungling of the national coronavirus response with what I expect Obama would have done. Going out on a limb here, but still...

Obama established the National Security Council Directorate for Global Health Security and Biodefense after the Ebola outbreak in 2016. Its mission: do everything possible to prepare for the next disease outbreak and prevent it from becoming an epidemic or pandemic.

The better the Directorate did its job, the less we would hear about it. Who publicizes an epidemic that doesn't happen or a health tragedy avoided? Not No-Drama-Obama.

Two years later, the Trump dissolved the Directorate.

When the 2020 coronavirus pandemic hit, the unprepared Trump administration, deprived of critical research, data, planning and coordination tools, mishandled the initial response. An interest rate cut to handle a deadly virus? Really?

This bungling guaranteed headline news and national fear, ensuring that anything short of national destruction gets labelled a victory. The Trump playbook to a T.

Let's go one step further. Imagine that Obama had pre-emptively implemented aggressive programs to keep Americans safe:

- Had he terminated airline passenger arrivals from Europe (like Trump did), Fox News would have screamed 'government overreach'.

- Had he closed public schools for a month (like several mayors and governors have), House Republicans would have screamed 'nanny state' and sought a court injunction.

- Had he waived interest on government supplied student loans and promised free coronavirus testing for all Americans (like

Trump did), Senator Lindsay Graham would have shrieked 'socialism'.

- And the list goes on.

Interestingly, George Bernard Shaw, the great Irish playwright, commented on all this in his 1906 play, the Doctor's Dilemma:

- "When men die of disease, they are said to die from natural causes." Translation: if Trump's policies fail, it's because COVID-19 was unstoppable. An easily available and credible excuse since the initial government response was so badly bungled and late.

But

- "When they recover (and they mostly do) the doctor gets the credit of curing them." Translation: if our country avoids total destruction, it's because of Trump's interventions.

Imagine Trump's victory speech, and he'll certainly give one: 'Through my decisive actions, I kept the US death toll down to 200.'

> Or 2000.
>
> Or 20,000.
>
> Or 200,000.
>
> Or 2,000,000.

The number doesn't matter to Trump. The country recovered. People returned to work. The stock market rose. He won.

Shaw accused doctors who mistreat patients for their own gain of having "no honor and no conscience".

I'd apply the same label to our current administration.

- It cut public health spending thus putting us more at risk.

- It eliminated critical biodefense departments thus depriving us of advanced warning and planning.
- It destroyed people's lives and economic well-being through poor execution.

It will then claim victory.

I think Shaw nailed it.

Unfortunately for us all.

Gary Fradin

Beating Covid?

We all hope the country will reopen soon, possibly June or July and then we'll adjust to a new post-Covid normal.

We'll go out again, eat out again, shop again, commute again and work again but in less crowded businesses and offices.

While I hope this rosy future occurs, I question the optimism for two main reasons.

First, even if the US defeats Covid-19, the rest of the world won't. Think about the 3+ billion people living in countries with minimal public health resources or social distancing opportunities, countries like Nigeria, Mexico, Bangladesh, Guatemala and Chad.

We're too intertwined to ignore their plight. People migrate. Products flow. Viruses transmit. A plague that affects them will somehow affect us.

I lived in Chad for 2 years in the 1970s. Chad then had a hospital. Now it has 15 million people and .05 doctors per 1000 of them.

The US has 2.6 per 1000, 52 times as many.

Chadian doctors in those days had bandages, aspirin, tongue depressors and rudimentary surgical supplies. The one hospital overflowed with patients, most in hallways. It had no food service, little sanitation and frequently reused 'single use' syringes. That was during a non-epidemic.

How can facilities like these defeat Covid?

Or Guatemala, 17 million people with .04 docs / 1000 people. 60% of Guatemalans live below the poverty level. Half the kids are chronically malnourished.

I spoke last February with a Guatemalan tour guide / teacher who explained why Guatemalans come to the US, typically as illegal immigrants despite the risks.

'We know' he explained, 'that 15% of us will die en route. We know how difficult life is for an illegal in the US. I have a brother and sister living there illegally. They tell me everything.

For us, those migration and undocumented risks are worth taking.

If we stay here, our kids starve.'

That was before Covid, before Guatemala's tiny health system tried to tackle the pandemic.

Now multiply Chad and Guatemala by 20 or 30 and remember that what happens in Guatemala doesn't stay in Guatemala.

We can't isolate our entire country from the world. Just imagine our economy with no imports or exports. That's depression with a capital D, plus, likely, hyperinflation.

'Well', say some, 'we'll vaccinate our way out.'

Which brings us to problem #2, the hoped-for vaccines.

I'm skeptical.

The experts say we'll have a vaccine in 12 – 18 months. Assume they're right.

That timing allows only a few months for human testing to see how well the vaccines actually work in real life. Will they be 80% effective? 70%? 50%?

Full disclosure about me: I'm not an anti-vaccine guy and I study medical quality for a living.

Those new anti-Covid vaccines will stay in our systems for years. We assume – hope – that the impact, both positive and negative, in year 4 will be the same as in month 4.

Valid assumption? Don't know.

How well will the vaccines work? Don't know.

For how long? Don't know.

What happens if / when the virus mutates? Don't know.

What are the long term, say 5 or 10 year harms? Don't know.

What happens in 2022 if, say, 80% of Americans are vaccinated with an 80% effective vaccine yet the world contains 3 billion at risk people? I shudder to think both medically and economically.

Yes, at some point we'll beat Covid.

I'd bet on it.

But I wouldn't bet on normal returning anytime soon.

*****

Editors note: this was published in approximately April, 2020. Covid vaccinations became widespread in February, 2021.

Gary Fradin

Saying 'Stop'

Trump supporters - about 130 million Americans – never say 'Stop. I'm outraged. You've gone too far.'

They didn't say 'stop' when Trump described Mexican-Americans as drug dealers, murderers, rapists and killers in 2015. He became the most popular Republican running for President within a month.

They didn't say 'stop' when he called for a 'total and complete shutdown of Muslims entering the United States' in 2015. His approval rose to 41%.

They didn't say 'stop' when he described the 'very fine people' at the Charlottesville 2017 'Unite the Right' rally organized by neo-Confederates, neo-fascists, white nationalists, neo-Nazis, Klansmen and right-wing militias chanting 'Jews will not replace us'. His approval 'slumped' to 39% of Americans.

They didn't say 'stop' when he told several black and brown members of Congress to 'go back' to their home countries even though all were American citizens. His approval remained at 40%.

They didn't say 'stop' when he attacked individuals like Mika Brzezinski, Bruce Ohr, Bob Corker, Lisa Page, Gonzalo Curiel, Andrew McCabe, Brent Bozell, John Brennan, Jean Carroll, Peter Strzok, Rex Tillerson, Katy Tur or dozens of others by name even though none were ever charged with or convicted of crimes.

Instead of 'stop', his supporters say 'I didn't really see it', Senator Ron Johnson on tear gassing demonstrators in Lincoln Park so Trump could have a photo-op.

'I'm late for lunch' Senator Rob Portman, commenting on the same event.

'I'm not going to critique other people's performances', Senator Mitch McConnell.

Or, most upsettingly, 'he speaks for me'.

How can we understand this failure of otherwise decent Americans to say 'stop' to racism, divisiveness and hate?

How do we understand the disconnect between the personal kindness shown by typical Trump supporters and their public support of Trump's obnoxious evilness?

And, at a personal level, what happens if Trump attacks me – or you reader - for some reason or none? Will his supporters follow him?

As I pondered all this, I recalled a story my Dad told many years ago, late 1970s from foggy memory.

A professional colleague of his, German Jewish guy who fled alone as a teenager in the 1930s, had recently revisited his hometown. His parents had been murdered in concentration camps and his former neighbors welcomed him warmly, sadly reminiscing about his lost family and fondly remembering their good times together.

'We liked your parents very much and we miss them' or words to that effect.

One neighbor kindly invited him to lunch, which he graciously accepted.

But he walked out when he realized that lunch was served on his parent's cutlery, still monogramed with their initials!

His parent's murder created an opportunity for that 'kind' neighbor to plunder his house.

True story.

I see in Trump supporters the same dichotomy: personally often kind but publicly supporting hate.

While I thought of my Dad's story, the words from Martin Niemoller's famous poem came to mind, badly updated here:

'First they came for the Moslems, and I didn't say 'stop' because I was not a Moslem.'

'Then they came for the immigrants and I didn't say 'stop' because I was not an immigrant.'

'Then they came for the liberals...then the poor...then the Press...then the Blacks...then the environmentalists...then the handicapped...'

'Then they came for me.'

People who don't say 'stop' to Trump's evilness diminish us all.

They really scare me.

I fervently hope they will finally, at long last, begin to say 'stop'.

Gary Fradin

Predicting the Presidential Election's October Surprise

Yogi Berra, or maybe Oscar Wilde, once said 'never make predictions, especially about the future'.

Bearing their caution in mind, I'll predict this October's election surprise.

Actually, since this election is about Donald Trump – not, unfortunately, about Joe Biden, the only decent, dependable, reasonable person running - I'll make 3 different predictions about Trump's behavior based on his mid-October polling.

If Trump leads by a lot and figures victory is in the bag his Justice Department will indict Joe Biden, or possibly son Hunter, on some nonsensical charge or other - assisting with the Benghazi coverup, influence peddling, Obamagate (whatever that is) or something equally inane.

The indictment flows from Trump's overall bully approach to life: when your opponent is down, kick him again.

Circle October 25 for the Biden indictment announcement.

The lack of factual basis for this matters not; only the headline news broadcast 24/7 on Fox News does. In Trumpworld, noise matters and a Biden indictment certainly creates noise.

If the polls are close in early October, Trump will launch a two-pronged surprise.

First, he'll announce a Covid-19 vaccine that is, in his words, 'perfect'. Maybe not as perfect as his shake-down phone call with Ukraine's Volodymyr Zelensky but perfect nonetheless.

The vaccine, of course, won't be perfect. It can't be. Normal vaccine testing takes 10 – 15 years.

Rushing the Covid-19 vaccine approval is like trying to create a baby in 1 month by getting 9 women pregnant. Can't happen.

But the announcement makes news headlines, the mother's milk of Trump's existence.

Second, he'll announce a military attack from Iran or North Korea, pick one, and declare war in return. I would guess Iran as it's militarily weaker. What bully would pick a fight with the stronger opponent?

Wars have historically boosted Presidential approval ratings so, Trump will figure, 'why not again now?'

Anyway, he's a wartime president, at least in his own mind.

A few extra votes from war fever – imaginary or not, doesn't matter as long as people believe it until November 3 – plus a few from the (imaginary) perfect vaccine should put him over the top.

Circle October 15 for the vaccine announcement and October 29 for the war declaration.

If Trump is far behind in mid-October, I predict he'll discover a disabling medical condition that requires him to drop out. Something incapacitating but not life threatening like bone spurs.

No, not bone spurs. He already used that one to avoid the Vietnam War.

Maybe a benign coronary event, rare blood condition, phlebitis (Nixon tried that in 1974), something that can resolve itself over time with treatment and rest.

Circle October 20 for the medical condition / drop out announcement.

Imagine Trump's nationally televised speech: 'My fellow Americans, I know that I will win this election next month because I'm a stable genius, the Fake News lies about polls and I have been the greatest President since Lincoln – actually, the greatest American since our country was founded after Washington defeated the British at Gettysburg - but on doctor's orders, I must withdraw my name from the ballot.'

Look at the upsides for Trump.

First, he doesn't lose. He hates losers.

Second, he retains his base, possibly for a future run. 'But for the health problems in 2020…..'

Third, after he recovers – no doubt faster than the doctors expect - he can pivot back to money-making, things like Trump TV.

Fourth, he retains the best parts of his Presidency – the rallies, adulation, prestige and hero-worship – without the responsibility.

One minor problem looms of course: he'll lose Presidential immunity, have to disclose his tax returns and likely face multiple state and federal lawsuits. But his lawyers can drag that out for years.

But hey - maybe he can make a deal with Biden! (Sorry Jared, you're on your own with that 666 Fifth Avenue refinance.)

The saddest parts of all this are that Trump – a con artist and ignoramus - actually gets to play with the Presidential election this way.

And that a formerly proud political party will embrace whatever sleaze he perpetrates.

Will the election actually play one of these ways? We'll know by November 4.

Gary Fradin

I'm a Conservative

It turns out, after reviewing my positions, that on many issues I'm a classic conservative.

I like balanced budgets, free trade, international organizations, law-and-order and honesty from our elected leaders.

I support my local police force even, albeit rarely, taking baked goods to the station. I like neighborhood primary schools, believe strongly in the separation of Church and State and think the doctor-patient relationship is key to a good healthcare system.

Maybe I should be a Republican!

Not a chance.

Let me explain.

Balanced budgets force us to live within our means and avoid having future generations pay for current consumption. Only in rare circumstances like economic depressions or major infrastructure expansions, should we finance current consumption with our children's dollars.

By contrast, the 2017 Republican tax-cuts-to-keep-a-strong-economy-going exploded our deficit, adding $2 trillion in debt while reducing unemployment from 4.1% in November 2017 to 3.8% in March 2019 with no structural economic improvements.

That forces future generations to fund today's TV, kitchen and vacation purchases - a classic economic sugar high with atrocious intergenerational morality.

Free trade brings down goods and service costs and stimulates economic cooperation around the world. This rewards, if done appropriately, both workers and consumers.

Today's Republicans reject all this in favor of trade barriers that harm both consumers (higher prices) and workers (lower wages).

Bad economics and particularly harmful to the most economically vulnerable among us.

I support **strong international institutions** like the United Nations, North America Free Trade Agreement, NATO, Trans Pacific Partnership and the Paris Climate Accord.

Though flawed, they have generally improved living standards, maintained world peace and fostered international cooperation.

Today's Republicans have exited some of these treaties and reduced our participation in others without any replacement alternative except machismo.

That's reimagined 19th century gunboat diplomacy not 21st century leadership, about a century out-of-date.

I strongly endorse **law-and-order** for both blue and white collar crimes, especially when done compassionately.

Vandalize someone's house and get punished. Lie on your income taxes and get sanctioned. Lie about your product's safety and go to jail.

Undermine the US election process and go to jail for a long time.

Today's Republicans seem happy to prosecute blue collar crime but loathe to prosecute white collar. Think campaign finance violations, witness tampering, pardons for Joe Arpaio, Scooter Libby and Conrad Black, obstruction of justice or violations of the Constitution's emoluments clause… and that's just Donald Trump.

I want the State out of my **religious activities** as I want it out of my **medical decisions**. I trust my own religious and medical advisors for guidance, not soundbite driven politicians trying to impose their medieval beliefs on me.

I strongly believe in traditional American values like **honesty**.…

I'm an old softee for 'my word is my bond' and abhor having a liar, thief and misogynist as President.

...and **patriotism**.

I simply can't understand how a political party calls itself patriotic without being outraged at the cyber- attacks on our electoral system. Nor can I understand supporting a leader who refuses even to talk about it.

As a conservative American, I cannot countenance the Republican party. I reject their preferences for deficit funding, trade barriers, go-alone foreign policy, conflation of Church with State, lack of patriotism and embrace of a liar as leader.

Today's Republicans don't stand for what makes America great.

They stand for what makes America worse.

Gary Fradin

Why Black Lives Matter to Everyone

Making Black lives matter generates huge benefits for all Americans according to extensive medical and public health research.

Consider 3 major studies.

First, the Whitehall studies, the original research into social determinants of health, showed that the lower your socio-economic status, the higher your disease rates and the shorter your life expectancy.

And the converse: the higher your socio-economic status, the less you cost medically.

In this country, African Americans are disproportionally poor. Higher disease rates among poor people drive up everyone's healthcare costs.

As those costs rise, compliance rates with medical prescriptions fall. Americans are, largely for cost reasons today, less likely than western Europeans to follow their doctor's orders, take their daily medications and refill prescriptions on schedule. Everyone's health suffers.

Plus healthcare is increasingly unaffordable.

Black lives matter to everyone who wants to control healthcare spending.

Second, consider the 2013 Institute of Medicine's 'US Health in International Perspective.'

It found that well insured, college educated, wealthy Americans have worse health than similarly educated and wealthy folks in other advanced, industrialized countries like Canada, Britain and France.

Among the reasons: the US has poorer public health systems and living environments. COVID-19 highlighted these problems.

'Public health' means safe public parks, good public transportation, clear air and water, effective preschools, drug and alcohol abuse prevention, widespread vaccinations and the like, all areas in which the US lags. These, far more than private medical care, reduce disease rates and promote longevity.

A well funded public health system that improves Black lives through better public transportation, better drug abuse prevention, safer public parks and cleaner drinking water will dramatically also help everyone else.

And third, Deaths of Despair by Anne Case and Nobel laureate Angus Deaton found that death rates among white Americans age 45 – 54 have *risen* in recent years, especially white men without a college degree. This has not happened in other countries.

The main causes are substance abuse, alcohol related diseases and suicide, formerly predominantly diseases of minority communities.

Non college educated white American longevity has now fallen to rival African American.

Quick summary:

- Poor people cost more medically which affects everyone's health costs.
- Low public health investments harm us all.
- Diseases of despair harm increasing numbers of us.

Making Black lives matter can address all these problems and benefit us all.

I wonder, though, if we will finally believe both the moral imperative to treat people decently and the medical research that shows a positive impact from doing so.

I certainly hope so.

For all our sakes.

With all due respect...

Words in context often mean the opposite of words in a dictionary.

'With all due respect' means 'I don't respect'.

'Don't worry' means 'worry' as, for example, when uttered by a teenager to a parent.

'The check's in the mail' means 'I haven't paid' and 'I'm from the government and I'm here to help' means…well, you get the idea.

Let's look at some political comments paraphrased here for brevity, and guess who said which below.

'I believe in having a strong family and real values' means 'I change wives when I get tired of them' and 'I demand pre-nuptial agreements from wives and non-disclosure agreements from family members'.

'We won't consider a Supreme Court nominee before an election' means 'we'd fill a Supreme Court vacancy before an election'.

'I don't like the idea of injecting bad stuff in your body' as in vaccines means 'I like the idea of injecting live coronavirus in your body' as in vaccines.

'He doesn't represent my Party' means 'I vote with him 87% of the time'.

'I'm a stable genius' means 'I brag to cover up my academic deficiencies' and 'I went to the best schools' means 'I brag to cover up my academic deficiencies'. As the old saying goes, 'if you have to tell someone you're smart, then you know you aren't' which means 'if you have to tell someone you're smart, then you know you aren't'.

'The failing New York Times' means 'I wish they would write something nice about me'.

'Fake News' means 'I wish they would write something nice about me'.

'You're a terrible reporter' means 'I wish you would write something nice about me'.

'I do solemnly swear that I will support and defend the Constitution of the United States against all enemies, foreign and domestic' means 'I will do everything I can to hold power regardless of what the Constitution or other laws say'.

Rather than believing the words themselves, consider the speaker's character; this speaks volumes while dictionary definitions are often ephemeral or circumstantial.

People with good character occasionally misspeak while people with poor character speak to misdirect.

Who and what you choose to believe is, of course, up to you.

Stealing Signs

Someone stole my Black Lives Matter sign last month.

They deliberately walked 15 yards across my lawn one night and took it.

I was angry. _My_ sign on _my_ lawn.

For saying the same things as LeBron James, Mitt Romney, Roger Goodell, the NBA and Major League Baseball.

For posting the same sign as Holy Trinity Lutheran Church up the street.

Then last night my 'We Believe' sign was taken.

Vandalism, again, of my personal property for expressing an opinion.

Outrageous.

My anger, soon merged with annoyance at the thief's childishness.

We used to tell our kids not to take other kid's stuff and to use words when upset. My thief apparently never learned those fundamental lessons. So puerile.

I then thought about our society at large. I'm upset that we can't express our political or social beliefs without fear of vandalism or violence, of retribution by people who disagree.

I tried this thought experiment: would I worry about personal harm if I posted a Republican position on my lawn? Something positive about Trump or inane like 'No Socialism Here'.

No, I decided. No concern about violence.

Only concerned that my thoughtful friends would think less of me.

Then I wondered about posting a Democratic sign on my lawn, something positive about Biden or Black Lives Matter.

We know the result.

My takeaway is that one side - the pro-Trump - resorts to theft, vandalism and violence more commonly than moderates and progressives. Local evidence supports this conclusion: 40 Black Lives Matter signs were lifted around town in the past few weeks compared to 2 pro-Trump ones.

That 20-to-1 ratio strikes me as about right.

My other takeaway is that the anti-BLM folks are surprisingly insecure. Their reaction to a little sign speaks volumes.

Anti-BLM folks apparently fear a loss of social and political standing as we become a majority-minority country. The more equality Blacks gain, they insecurely figure, the less they retain for themselves.

My Black Lives Matter sign brings home this self-perceived marginality. It becomes something anti-BLMers have to destroy before – horrors – other people might see it.

So they steal it at night, pathetically trying to make themselves feel better, pathetically trying to hide their fragility and pathetically unsuccessful at both.

I'm angry about the vandalism.

I'm disappointed that the anti-BLM folks feel such a need to go low.

I'm upset that our society has deteriorated so profoundly that we resort to adolescent petulance as political expression.

And I worry that sign stealing is but a precursor of things to come.

What Would Mussolini Say?

Benito Mussolini would be impressed with Donald Trump.

Mussolini, Italy's Fascist Party founder, ideologue, leader and disastrous Prime Minister from 1922 – 1943, defined fascism as the merger of state and corporate power. Citizens for him exist primarily to serve that marriage of political and corporate power we call government.

Fascist leaders follow a standard playbook: appease supporters by delivering safety and order then build nationalist cohesion by labelling vulnerable minorities as 'outsiders' and attacking them. Think historically of gypsies and Jews, today of immigrants and Blacks, anyone racially different enough from the nationalist self-image to ostracize.

Fascists, per Mussolini, have contempt for democracy, subordinate individualism to community interests and worship a leader whose persona equates with the state.

As I watch the Trump administration call for law-and-order, I think of that fascist racial playbook.

As I watched the 4-day Republican supplication to Donald Trump called their National Convention, I saw the leader's persona equated with the state.

As I watch them upend norms, decency and laws – underfunding the Post Office to reduce voting by mail during a pandemic, firing Inspectors General for uncovering corruption, labelling the media as enemies of the people, flaunting rules when appointing senior officials and playing coy with relinquishing power if Trump loses the election – I think of Mussolini's contempt for democracy.

And as I watch the stock market rise along with lobbying power, unemployment and income inequality, I see us all becoming subservient to the state - corporate monolith.

Consider these data points about income inequality and corporate power:

Some 10% of US households own 85% of the stocks owned by Americans.

About 400 very wealthy people – those stock owners - donated half the money raised in the 2016 election cycle.

Today the stock market soars benefitting these folks while over 30 million of us are unemployed and countless more underemployed.

Meanwhile the government increasingly abandons its public safety function, enhancing corporate-political power instead. Trump's EPA, for example, weakened greenhouse gas emission restraints from coal plants at the bequest of coal companies for profits and votes. Health consequences ignored.

His EPA reduced prosecutions of polluters to the lowest rate in 30 years, about a quarter as many as Clinton, to appease corporate polluters despite the public health cost.

His legislative arm, the Republican party, recently proposed restrictions on suing nursing homes for negligence despite many homes having poor safety records. Corporate profits and campaign contributions again. Sorry your mother died but it is what it is.

Our best Presidents fought against this. Harry Truman, an anti-fascist if ever there was one, defined the President's job this way in the 1940s:

"There are 14 or 15 million Americans who have the resources to have representatives in Washington to protect their interests, and the interests of the great mass of the other people - the 150 or 160 million - is the responsibility of the President of the United States."

Donald Trump and his enablers believe exactly the opposite, that the President should protect corporate power, that workers exist to increase corporate profits and that the great mass of Americans exist to support him.

Trump's appointments and policies show how closely today's corporations have merged with government and his law-and-order platform embodies the fascist playbook as we increasingly descend into Mussolini's dystopian vision.

Mussolini would certainly shout 'bravo' if he could see Trump in action.

Gary Fradin

Protecting Pre-existing Conditions?

President Trump and his supporters want to repeal the Affordable Care Act and 'protect pre-existing conditions'. I don't understand this. And I study healthcare for a living.

'Protect pre-existing conditions' seems to mean 'people with chronic medical conditions will retain access to health insurance'.

This becomes important if the ACA's coverage guarantees disappear. Insurers – private, often for-profit companies constantly seeking ways to lower their medical payout – like to restrict or eliminate coverage of high cost subscribers. They have done this regularly, historically.

'Protect pre-existing conditions' theoretically forces insurers to cover everyone. What problems might this entail?

We'll start with access issues. Will people with pre-existing conditions have access to...

The same health insurance plans as people without?

The same premiums?

Plans without waiting periods, i.e. 60 or 180 day (or longer) periods without insurance coverage?

Plans without carve-outs, i.e. insurance exceptions related to your pre-existing condition?

Plans without annual or lifetime caps?

The list of access questions becomes endless. Answers are simultaneously unavailable and critically important to the 54 million non-elderly Americans affected.

Second, let's attempt to define 'pre-existing conditions', something that no one, let alone our Republican repeal-and-replace advocates have done; there's no clear, comprehensible, universally accepted definition.

The US Department of Health and Human Services, for example, defines pre-existing conditions as 'health problems you had before the date your new coverage starts', a Swiss-cheese definition at best.

Which of the following qualify, if any?

> Pregnancy
> Coronavirus
> Alcoholism
> Psoriasis
> Insomnia
> Irritable bowel syndrome
> Breast cancer, successfully treated 8 years ago
> Blood pressure of 150/100...or 145/95...or 140/90
> Body Mass Index of 28....or 29...or 30....or 31. What's the cut-off?

The potential list is endless.

Third, let's ask how we decide what qualifies as a pre-existing condition. This matters because of the potential numbers of people and dollars at stake.

Trump and the Republicans seem to favor 'high risk pools' of money that folks with pre-existing conditions can access to purchase health insurance. Under the vaguely defined program, each state would get money from the Federal government to fund these pools.

Pre-existing condition definitions might become state dependent. Pregnancy, for example, might be a pre-existing condition in some states but not others.

Ditto blood pressure. Imagine one state defining 130/85 as a pre-existing condition, another using 160/110 as the cut-off and other states in between.

More concerningly, though, budget pressure would create incentives for the Feds to reduce high risk pool funding over time with unclear insurance and medical repercussions.

Might people have pre-existing condition subsidies for years, then lose them? Unclear.

Do people with pre-existing conditions who lose their subsidies also lose any other protections? Unclear.

How might labelling someone as having a pre-existing condition affect their health insurance access and premiums in the future? Unclear again.

As I look at the 'protect pre-existing conditions' quagmire, I think about the insurance access problems, the definitional problems and the funding problems. Any individually would concern me; all three together scare me.

There is some good news though for people in Massachusetts. Our state laws guarantee equal health insurance access for all residents regardless of medical condition. Whether the ACA goes or stays and whether we proceed nationally with Trump's so-called pre-existing condition protections, we in Massachusetts as relatively safe on the health insurance access front.

For that, Massachusetts residents can thank our enlightened voters and the resulting high quality leaders we elect.

Gary Fradin

Do Massachusetts Democrats Eat Their Old?

Some in the animal kingdom, like cats, prairie dogs and birds, eat their young to conserve precious resources and help their species survive.

Massachusetts Democrats, on the other hand, apparently eat their old to protect noblesse oblige.

I can't think of any other reason to justify Joe Kennedy's quest to unseat Ed Markey.

Kennedy, a fine, hard working and reliable though undistinguished Congressman, claims we need a change because 'our country's hurting' according to his TV ads and 'we need relief' ...before launching into the standard progressive agenda, essentially Ed Markey's platform.

Another TV ad says he wants to build something better, something stronger for the future, something I suspect like the Green New Deal sponsored by... Ed Markey.

Joe sounds like Ed with a more cosmopolitan accent!

Markey has certainly performed well enough to justify reelection. He's solidly progressive and increasingly senior which, under the Senate's arcane rules, means increasingly powerful. Why substitute the less powerful voice for the more powerful when they say the same things?

I'll postulate 3 reasons - 2 good and 1 bad - for replacing a political incumbent.

First, the incumbent might represent his or her constituents poorly. Doesn't apply to Markey.

Second, the challenger might be incredibly outstanding and present future prospects that the incumbent could never achieve. Think of Barak Obama as a young senator or maybe AOC or Ayanna Presley in Congress, galvanizing voters with their passion, vision, charisma and personal stories.

Though I like Joe, this doesn't apply to him..

We're left with the bad reason to replace an incumbent - noblesse oblige. "I'm young and fresh. My great uncle was a Senator from Massachusetts and President of the United States, my other great uncle was the longest serving Senator from Massachusetts, my grandfather was a Senator from New York and now it's my turn".

I'd object to this equally from a Bush, Romney, Rockefeller, Sunnu or Trump.

It says that the son of a milkman can hold political power only until a young noble decides it's his turn. It tells middle class kids thinking about political careers - sons and daughters of teachers and social workers, plumbers and cops – that they can only go as far as the nobility allows.

I like having Joe in Congress and Ed in the Senate, both representing Massachusetts well.

Too bad we have to cannibalize our DC representation and maybe start from scratch on two seniority ladders just to satisfy one man's ego and self perceived destiny.

Has Our National Experiment Run Its Course?

Most of us today claim to be patriotically American but define 'American' differently, typically as 'people sharing our values and viewpoints,' often with a strong regional component.

Massachusetts residents, for example, tend to embrace Democratic party values while Kentucky voters embrace Republican, voting Red in national elections about as consistently as we vote Blue.

These two tribes, the Blues and Reds – often regionally defined - hold very different world views with a chasm in between. Consider these exit polls from earlier this month.

93% of Republicans think the country is heading in the right direction; 79% of Democrats say the wrong direction.

86% of Republicans want to repeal the Affordable Care Act; 83% of Democrats want to save or expand it.

85% of Republicans want to build a wall on the Mexican border; 85% of Democrats oppose.

The top 3 issues for Republican voters: economy, immigration, law enforcement.

The top 3 issues for Democratic voters: climate change, racism, Covid.

Where's the national common ground ... issue #27?

Colin Woodward, author of "American Nations: A History of the Eleven Rival Regional Cultures in North America", argues provocatively that American regions are so culturally diverse that they're each almost separate nations, making it difficult to build a true national, popular consensus.

To oversimplify, Woodward says New Englanders value education, intellectual achievement and communal empowerment, feel comfortable with government regulation and have a utopian streak.

Appalachians, on the other hand, states like Kentucky, Tennessee and Arkansas, value personal sovereignty and individual liberty, education far less than us, are suspicious of the federal government and lack that utopian streak.

I find Woodward intriguing and the implications both upsetting and conceivable.

Imagine that New Englanders form an independent country, the United States of New England, defined by universal healthcare, free public college tuition, green energy and a knowledge-based economy.

New England could fund the desired public programs with the $20+ billion it currently loses in federal taxes, the difference between what it paid last year and what it got back. As one example, Massachusetts residents paid $13,820 on average in federal taxes but only got $11,477 back.

Kentucky, by contrast, received back $15,897 per resident from the feds but only paid in $6,752 on average.

In other words, enlightened (my word) Massachusetts residents subsidize unenlightened (my word again) Kentucky residents AND try to persuade them to accept our progressive values AND THEN compromise with them on critical policies like the Covid response, healthcare, climate, energy, equality and education financing.

The United States of New England would still, of course, trade with the other states like currently with Canada; economic integration does not require political integration. New England could sell Kentucky biotechnology and educational services, buy back bourbon and coal. (Who wants their coal?)

As the social and cultural fabric of America frays today under the onslaught of biased news, alternative facts, widespread cynicism and Trumpian authoritarianism, I find myself wondering about this type of future.

I wonder not only ***if*** Joe Biden can bring us together but ***whether he should***. Are the costs of national unity too high these days? Is the goal of national unity even realistic anymore? For the first time in my life, my answer is 'I'm not sure'.

Maybe our grand national experiment in shared values has run its course.

Maybe we're too big, too diverse, too distrustful of each other and too regionally defined to make national consensus either possible or meaningful.

Maybe regional affiliations actually lie at our core.

Maybe that's, in fact, the true future path for America.

Gary Fradin

Can Our House Divided Against Itself Continue to Stand?

A house divided against itself cannot stand. So famously said Abraham Lincoln in 1858.

America is pretty divided today. 2/3 of Democrats and Republicans would oppose a family member marrying the other political party according to recent surveys, up from 5% in 1960.

Our two political parties have become pseudo-religions, complete with **belief systems** – Democrats believe in inclusive communities and equality, Republicans in individual responsibility and law-and-order - **rituals** – Republicans carry guns, Democrats drive Priuses – and **values** – Republicans oppose abortion, Democrats favor choice.

Today's Democrats and Republicans not only lack a shared vision for America, but both increasingly distrust and despise the other. To that end, both have built communication cathedrals to spread their opposing gospels, with Republicans far more effective.

Sean Hannity, Rush Limbaugh, Tucker Carlson and Laura Ingraham proselytize like Savonarola, Josef Goebbels and Father Charles Coughlin in the past, finding evil Democratic conspiracies under every stone and rallying the faithful against undesirables - intellectuals, liberals, ethnic minorities, racial minorities, internationalists, environmentalists and more – with emotionally toxic, factually challenged daily sermons.

They know that facts matter less to committed believers than outrage.

How factually challenged are these orators? US District Court Judge Mary Kay Vyskocil, a Trump appointee, recently ruled that Fox's Carlson engages in "bloviating for the audience" even when saying 'these are the facts.' (I'm not making this up.)

Fox's own defense lawyers argued in court that Carlson can't slander people in any legal sense because he "is not stating actual facts about the topics he discusses" (direct quote), this prime time on a so-called news network.

How emotionally toxic is all this? Studies show that anger can become addicting. Perceived or imaged threats – 'the Democrats will take away your liberties' or 'socialism is just around the corner' – stimulate adrenaline and dopamine, a 'feel good' hormone in our brains. "People get a literal rush from getting angry," according to psychiatrist Dr. Jean Kim. It "feels good. You end up liking it."

"Anger, fear, moral indignation, these types of things are the news equivalents of what we see in the entertainment industry — sex and violence," according to Sarah Sobieraj of Tufts University who studies this stuff.

Rather than educating audiences, non-fact demagogues provide pseudo information mixed with outrage to give exasperated viewers their daily dopamine fix.

The unfortunate result: a poorly informed, factually challenged national population certain that 'we're right and the other side is trying to destroy America'.

This – frighteningly - reminds me of Albert Camus' warning years ago about "ignorance that fancies it knows everything and therefore claims for itself the right to kill."

I fear for our future.

In today's America of bloviators generating adrenaline rushes and certainty, we have 270 million civilian guns and only a 30% positive view of the federal government.

We have one political party entirely tied to our truth-challenged, financially labile President who the other sees as evil.

We have a President telling armed supporters to "stand by" on national TV.

We have young Americans asking their parents if it's time to buy a gun to protect themselves after a nationally televised Presidential debate.

And we have a widespread public belief that America is in decline, entirely caused by the other side of our shakily standing house.

I don't know for how long our house can remain standing.

I fervently hope Joe Biden can rebuild it and make America a safe home for us all.

But I'm not sure he can.

Gary Fradin

The 'Republican Leaders' Oxymoron

Oxymorons are contradictory words used together like 'deafening silence'.

Examples include 'act naturally', 'bittersweet', 'small crowd', 'open secret' and, in America today, 'Republican leaders'.

Leaders 'act as a guide' and 'show the way' per dictionary.com. Leaders typically show courage, patriotism, integrity, civility and character.

Republican 'leaders' today? Hardly.

Exhibit 1, leadership and integrity. Carl Bernstein, the reporter who broke the Watergate story 50 years ago, recently tweeted a list of 21 Republican Senators who privately oppose - 'have extreme contempt for' - Trump behind doors but lack the integrity to state this publicly.

His list includes Republican Senate 'leaders' Whip John Thune and his predecessor John Cornyn, Senate GOP #4 Roy Blunt and National Republican Senatorial Committee Chair Rick Scott.

Saying one thing in private and another in public isn't leadership. It's hypocrisy, 'claiming to have moral standards or beliefs to which one's own behavior does not conform'.

Are Thune, Cornyn, Blunt, Scott and the others 'leaders' – guides to the future, or 'hypocrites' – folks who say one thing but act differently?

Embarrassingly easy to answer.

Exhibit 2 leadership and patriotism. Some 126 House Republicans joined the baseless lawsuit filed by 18 Republican attorneys general to overturn the last election.

That the US Supreme Court deemed this suit unworthy of consideration misses the point.

These Republican 'leaders' apparently think election results certified by each state are meaningless, thus overturning centuries of US practice and election law. The baseless lawsuit joiners included House minority leader Kevin McCarthy, the guy who will run the House if Republicans gain majority.

Patriotism for McCarthy and this crew apparently means 'disregard elections if you don't win'.

Disregard secretary of state certifications.

Disregard governor's certifications.

Disregard state voting laws after the fact.

And disregard the 40+ challenges already thrown out of court for, according to one judge, the 'flimsy foundation' that "would do indelible damage to every future election".

One wonders what patriotism means Republican 'leaders' like McCarthy. Apparently not 'abiding by election results as certified by every state'.

Exhibit 3, leadership and civility. McCarthy along with Senate Majority Leader Mitch McConnell refused to attend Ruth Bader Ginsburg's lie-in-state ceremony in the Capitol despite receiving an official invitation.

Decorum, decency and respect for the first woman in US history ever to receive such an honor are qualities apparently foreign to Republican 'leaders'.

I hate to guess the lesson they intend this (non)action to teach.

Exhibit 4, leadership, competence and public policy. Every 50 or so seconds, an American dies of Covid. That's almost as many as died in the 9/11 attacks...each day.

But President Trump gave no national speeches (think of 'we have nothing to fear but fear itself' from FDR), offered no inspiration (think of 'Ich bin ein Berliner' from John Kennedy) and proposed little national guidance including about vaccine distribution. A Pfizer spokesman actually said on December 18 "We have millions more doses sitting in our warehouse but, as of now, we have not received any shipment instructions".

Trump, meanwhile, tweeted some nonsense or other.

Republican national 'leadership' against Covid? Doesn't pass the smell test.

Exhibit 5, leadership and character. Our 45th President lacks the 'moral and ethical quality' - dictionary definition of character - to acknowledge reality and even say 'President-Elect Biden'.

He is characterologically unable to assist in the peaceful transfer of power, a hallmark of American democracy for 200+ years.

Vice President Pence, meanwhile, plans an overseas trip to avoid Biden's inauguration.

Leadership? More like pathetic, 'miserably inadequate' per the dictionary.

These two pathetic scoundrels symbolize the oxymoronic notion of Republican leadership today.

Gone from their lexicon are the thousand points of light.

Gone from their actions are the appeals to our greater angels.

Gone is the moral and ethical quality that once defined character.

No 'acting as a guide'.

No 'showing the way forward'.

No inspiring Americans to future greatness.

No working toward a more perfect union.

I hope the new year and new administration will allow and encourage Republicans to make their party great again. I really do. It will be good for them and good for America. I hope we can see it happen soon.

Gary Fradin

How NFL Coaches Might Explain Our Politics

Consider how these quotes from Dennis Greene, Vince Lombardi, Bill Parcels and Mike Tomlinson describe our politics today.

Cardinals Coach Dennis Greene: 'They are who we thought they were'. Greene described the Bears shortly after his Cardinals played them in 2009.

How much this sounds like today's Democrats saying 'Trump is who we thought he was', a self promoting, lying, authoritarian racist, interested only in his well being and utterly unconcerned about democracy, norms, public health, public institutions or public policy.

Trump is exactly who he claimed to be and anyone – from Mitch McConnell to Susan Collins, and Lindsay Graham to Mitt Romney - who thought they could tame, control, coddle or mollify this beast has been proven disastrously, undeniably and totally wrong.

He told us who he was.

But Republicans failed to listen and they, too, are who we thought they were, infinitely malleable, pandering sycophants…to their party's shame and our country's horror.

Packers Coach Vince Lombardi: 'Winning isn't everything, it's the only thing'.

The Packers legendary coach exactly described today's Republican election approach: suppress, challenge, discard and ignore votes unless you win.

Consider how multiple Republican Senators and Representatives objected to seating electors from 2020 swing states. The nonsensical justification according to Senator Josh Hawley: the Pennsylvania Supreme Court had incorrectly considered a voting rights lawsuit.

The Court, in other words, was wrong and Hawley uniquely knows what's right.

Today's Republicans want to litigate, litigate, litigate then litigate again and again until they get the desired outcome.

Law, norms, government certifications, recounts, court decisions and established rules don't matter.

Only winning matters. It's the only thing.

What a dismal way to poison our body politic.

Patriots Coach Bill Parcels: 'You are what your record says you are'.

I thought of this as Joe Biden and others said, after thugs broke into the Capitol, 'this is not who we are as a nation'.

No, according to Parcels' metric, this is exactly who we are, believers in strength, shouting and violence, followers of a deranged leader (at least half of us), people uninterested in supporting democracy, equality or law, unable to understand other points of view and unwilling to compromise for the greater good.

We are what our record says we are. And our record, at least recently, is pretty dismal.

Steelers Coach Mike Tomlinson: 'Excuses are the tools of the incompetent'.

The losing NFL coach doesn't ignore reality by shouting 'The ref stole the game with that bogus pass interference penalty' or 'My star players were injured – I demand a rematch'.

Instead after each NFL game the opposing coaches meet at midfield to shake hands, a tradition that means 'It's over and time to move on.'

Would that our political leaders had the character, grace and dignity of NFL coaches, an ability to live by the rules, accept reality and admit defeat when it comes.

Why don't they?

Because they are who we thought they were.

Winning is the only thing.

And we are what our record says we are.

Can We Return 2021 Within 30 Days for a Refund?
written on January 17, 2020

2021 started with promise, particularly on the morning of January 6 when news agencies called 2 Senate seats in Georgia for Democrats. Chuck Schumer, not Mitch McConnell, would set the Senate's agenda, Democrats would control Senate committees and thoughtful, progressive legislation became possible again.

Then that afternoon – unbelievably to rational, patriotic Americans - thugs inspired by Donald Trump and his allies, stormed the Capitol to stop Congress from certifying Joe Biden's win.

I don't know what will happen next, whether mob violence will shake our country on Inauguration Day, whether Joe Biden can bring us together or whether we will ever enjoy the pride of national unity again.

I don't know what this means for our children and grandchildren.

But I feel less safe, secure and proud of my country today than I did 2 weeks ago.

I'd like my money back for 2021. On balance, it has started disastrously.

I'd like to purchase 2022 instead.

Or 2023.

It can't be worse and might, I sincerely hope, be better.

Gary Fradin

Grandpa, What Did You Do During the Trump Years?

www.ingramcontent.com/pod-product-compliance
Lightning Source LLC
Chambersburg PA
CBHW021419210526
45463CB00001B/451